RECOGNISE YOUR LIGHT WITHIN
APNA MOOL PEHCHAN

PARMINDER SINGH SAHOTA

Printed in Great Britain by
Biddles Books Ltd, King's Lynn, Norfolk

Dedication

To my wife, Gursharan, and my children. Thank you for the unconditional love, limitless patience and the deep belief that every person can be nourished to being happy now. For showing me how to accept, with graciousness, every experience as a gift, an opportunity to get to know and love myself and you better. You are the example to which I endeavour to rise. That is my promise to you.

Thank you, Mehar, for planting the seed of this book within me. You said that the universe has a plan for everyone. If only we can pause for a moment and surrender, so that we may see.

I wear many hats, like everyone else. Husband, father, grandfather, son, friend, consultant – an endless list. I have played these roles with various degrees of success. That is how others defined me and how I defined myself. I still play these roles, and understand a little more now by drawing meaning through the experience of daily living. Anchored in a safe and deep harbour, I am still free to journey, with my Guru, the Siri Guru Granth Sahib Ji, as my guide and constant companion. Now I am much more than the roles I play. Not a noun anymore but an adjective – describing, through everyday living, the attributes of my Guru.

Parminder

Preface

ਫਰੀਦਾ ਦੁਨੀ ਵਜਾਈ ਵਜਦੀ ਤੂੰ ਭੀ ਵਜਹਿ ਨਾਲਿ ॥

"Farid, the world dances as it dances, and you dance with it as well."

ਸੋਈ ਜੀਉ ਨ ਵਜਦਾ ਜਿਸੁ ਅਲਹੁ ਕਰਦਾ ਸਾਰ

"That soul alone does not dance with it, who is under the care of the Lord God."
Salok Baba Sheikh Farid, 110.

Stop searching. What does it take to stop searching? A childhood in Thika (Kenya), university in Dayton, Ohio, and family life in Kenya and London. The excitement and pleasure of the party, the dance, the race, made life feel real. What else is there?

Being carefree due to indifference is not the same as being carefree because you are in the embrace of love. Saying "I know" because you have touched your horizon is not the same as saying it because you realise something more lies beyond.

It can just take a moment. The major heart attack at the age of 39 gave me moments. Barely alive, I realised that what I thought was important was not that which was sustaining me. Beyond my visible existence there was my soul. As my body almost stopped, I felt *me*, beyond my body. I saw the vast array of people, those I knew and those I did not, helping me. My wife's hand squeezing mine. The nurse's smile to comfort me. This *sewa* (selfless serving and living) of *sangat* (congregation) around me felt like the embrace of love. Nurtured and kept alive, my natural soul-being stood watching me, in the guise of Sikh spirits.

That which had sustained me showed itself faintly, for a moment; a deep sense of open-hearted gratitude, like a prayer, overcame me. I did not need to search. All I needed was always here. I was going to be fine.

This book is my story of arriving at what, I believe, sustains us all as individuals. It is written through the lens of Sikhism and, I would humbly suggest, is relevant to all of us.

Know yourself. *Apna mool pechan.* You will then see that what was previously invisible has been sustaining you all along. Commit to this through *sewa*, *simran* (constant practice of compassion, humility), *sangat* and *ardhas* (prayer). You will then stop searching for that which you have already.

ਚਾਰੇ ਕੁੰਡਾ ਢੂੰਢੀਆਂ ਰਹਣੁ ਕਿਥਾਊ ਨਾਹਿ

"I have searched in the four directions, but I have not found
any resting place anywhere."
Salok Baba Sheikh Farid, 102.

Contents

Introduction

After the heart attack: Seeking meaning to everyday life

Mool N Boojhai Aap N Soojhai Bharam Biaapee Ahan Manee

"Engrossed in doubt and egotism, [The mortal being] does
not know the Mool; he does not understand his own self."
(*Siri Guru Granth Sahib*)[1]

Einstein said: "There are two ways to live: you can live as if nothing
is a miracle; you can live as if everything is a miracle". For me,
still being here is a miracle. Although diagnosed with critical heart
failure, I suffer from no adverse symptoms such as breathlessness,
swollen ankles or fatigue. I have been told my heart has only a
20% function, meaning that only one-fifth of oxygenated blood is
pumped out of my heart to the rest of the body in every contraction.
I carry on with life as a normal, healthy person. I jog, swim, cycle
and exercise for extended periods without any physical discomfort
such as dizziness, fainting, confusion or wheezing.

I am just grateful to experience the daily miracles of living, such as
holding our grandchildren. Every time I begin to feel that I understand
what has brought me here, I see the journey ahead a little more
clearly and realise that I know even less than I thought. Still, it is a
wonderful journey and I enjoy the discovery and adventure.

It is amazing how we have abilities as humans to rise through
challenges and aspire to noble living which promotes our own total
well-being and that of others. The natural resources around us help
us to live rewarding lives. Does owning a lot make us "winners"

1 The Siri Granth Sahib is hereinafter abbreviated to "SGGS".

rather than "losers"? Many people live happily and purposefully with very little material wealth. For others, it is unimaginable. Maybe we can win together by being part of a connected community who give, receive and share so that everybody can gain opportunity and make progress. Easier said than done. We can win, but still feel a sense of loss. Martin Luther King, in his speech "Remaining Awake Through a Great Revolution" delivered at the National Cathedral in Washington, D.C. on 31 March 1968, reminded us that:

> One day we will have to stand before the God of history and we will talk in terms of things we've done. Yes, we will be able to say we built gargantuan bridges to span the seas, we built gigantic buildings to kiss the skies. Yes, we made our submarines to penetrate oceanic depths. We brought into being many other things with our scientific and technological power. It seems that I can hear the God of history saying, "That was not enough! But I was hungry, and ye fed me not. I was naked, and ye clothed me not. I was devoid of a decent sanitary house to live in, and ye provided no shelter for me. And consequently, you cannot enter the kingdom of greatness. If ye do it unto the least of these, my brethren, ye do it unto me." That's the question facing America today. (*Congressional Record*, 9 April 1968)

Critical heart failure and other life-changing events that remind us of our mortality have a way of making us dig deep and ask questions such as, "Why is my life this way?" "What have I become?" "Is this how I want to live my life?" The world outside only makes sense by looking at it from the world inside us ... our thoughts, feelings, understanding and perspectives. We need to make sure that our outer experiences connect with the world within us. Too often, we have followed how we imagine we are expected to live and not made decisions as we really wished.

This outward focus leads us down a path of confusion and eventual discontentment. Our own understanding of who we think we are gets blurred. Others close to us say they don't know who we are anymore.

That my days could end suddenly after an acute heart attack at 39 forced me to examine my life; to face myself honestly and appreciate all the gifts I receive every day.

I was shocked by the realisation that my life could end suddenly, and that all I had taken for granted and valued as important didn't matter anymore. The love and the compassion of my family aroused a torrent of emotions within me that varied from deep gratitude for the care and support being given to me to feelings of desperation about the distinct possibility that I had left returning this love far too late. Life can make you lose sight of the things that really matter. I had to be stripped bare emotionally and physically before I realised how much the people, the environment I lived in and the difference that I tried to make really mattered. Yes, I mattered too, because we all carry a light and have a contribution to make to the communal whole. It is the giving that helps us grow.

Alice Koller, author of the 1982 book *An Unknown Woman,* which explores the philosophical and psychological issues of self-identity expressed quite succinctly what I was feeling at that moment. "I've arrived at this outermost edge of my life," she says, "by my own actions. Where I am is thoroughly unacceptable. Therefore, I must stop doing what I've been doing." This had to be my very first step towards recovery.

On the treatment bed in the emergency ward, the shock and realisation that I might not last the day, the hour, or maybe even the next few minutes, drove and dragged me from deep gratitude for the care and support I was receiving to desperation and panic about my survival. I thought I knew my life; thought I knew me. Strangers mattered, too. The hospital staff were keeping me alive. Would I ever have the opportunity to thank them? What else was keeping me alive?

I was at a complete loss. Physically and emotionally bereft, I finally turned to my deepest solace. I had been brought up with the idea that what is in the universe is within us, and what is within us exists around us. I prayed for help to face up to the challenges ahead. At some point in the darkness of those early helpless days following the heart attack, I finally turned to my Guru and prayed for the support, strength and resilience to face up to the challenges ahead. It was all

I could reach for in order to survive. Now it became clear that I had to seek my Guru's grace. I had to affirm that life itself, with all its delights, was a fundamental gift.

Grace, ironically, also entails the possibility of ignoring the giver, the Guru, and making poor choices. By not choosing the most graceful path, I had ended up being confused and miserable.

Realising this predicament, was also an element of Guru's grace. Calling for his assistance, through *ardhas* (prayer), guided me back to the most graceful path. The Guru guided me onto a path that removed my self-conceit. This required faith and I suddenly had lots of it. Funny, how a life changing event, can give you faith. I am reminded, as I write this, of a saying by Rumi, a 13th-century Persian poet: "Oh my heart, don't become discouraged so easily. Have faith. In the hidden world, there are many mysteries, many wonders. Even if the whole planet threatens your life, don't let go of the Beloved's robe for even a breath." Just experiencing the moment of surrender or prayer took me towards looking at my life from a mountain top.

I saw more clearly that I had not lived my own life, but followed the crowd. Developed my habits, patterns and routines, but underestimated the importance of disciplined living. Looked at life around me, but seen mainly what I had wanted to see. Listened to try to learn, but still usually thought that I knew best. Enjoyed the comforts of life, but generally wanted for something else and more than I had.

I realised with regret and horror that, up to that point, I had led a life that seemed and felt mean and self-centred. I felt a sense of shame and desperation. Would I be able to correct this, I asked? This did seem like … me.

Now, with nowhere else to go, I bowed my head and surrendered to the uncertainty of being given what I needed rather than what I asked for. The *shabad* from the Sikh scriptures now comes to mind: "*Sagal dwar ko chad ke gayo tumharo dwar. Baan gaye ki laaj raas govind das tohar.*" ("I have left behind all the other doors and paths, and now (finally), I have come to your door. Take my arm and guide me, Lord, your servant.").

Little did I know that the door was in me. I had travelled to other sacred places, but not my own temple within. Saint Francis of Assisi, describing his own search for the divine, said: "I searched everywhere for you and realised you were where I was searching from". And Rumi echoed, "I kept on knocking on Your door and eventually realised I had been knocking from inside the door".

I prayed for the capacity to step up and get back onto my feet, both mentally and physically. I had faith in honest prayer. I recalled Sikh *shabads*: "*Jis ke sir upar tu swami so dukh kesa paaway*" ("With your hand upon me, Lord, how can suffering take me?") and "*Tu kahey dohley praania, tum rakey ga sirjan har*" ("Why do you lower your spirit, o man? God that has brought you here is not going to leave you now.").

I wept uncontrollably; but these tears were different. They were not tears of desperation, but tears of hope and joy from a sense of awakening to something bigger than me. I had heard these *shabads* countless times before, but never connecting, never understanding, never taking meaning from them. Now, effortlessly, something within me made sense of them – with clarity. Were my prayers said in humility and with faith this time? Does desperation give you faith and the humility to face yourself? I realised in that moment that my arrogance had not just been directed at others, but it was who I had become.

At that moment, for the first time in my life, I looked at my wife and actually saw her. When I saw her for who she was to me, the love I felt for her only reinforced the awakening. I was grateful she had stuck with me through all the turmoil and challenges I had put her through. Isn't it Mark Twain, the American author and humourist, who said, "Grief can take care of itself; but to get the full value of a joy you must have someone to divide it with"? How apt, I thought, and why is it that we are blind to things that are always with us?

What a wonderful insight. If only I had known this before. I wouldn't have put on all those different masks of pretence, believing the pretence as true, that I was a humble human being looking out for the good of others. We have the gift of rationalising all our thoughts and actions. We like to be seen doing the right thing. We seek to feel complete inside. To feel good inside. Even only for a short time. We call it happiness. Being happy. Even if it means hurting others. And the sad thing is we do this most of the time, unconsciously. We become the antithesis of who we think we are, who we make ourselves to be. Humility, my foot. I had never been anywhere near the meaning of the word. All pretence. Being timid. At that moment, I couldn't have been more ashamed of who I had become.

In a fleeting moment, I rationalised, yet again. Old habits don't die, they say. I rationalised that I had been looking for a purpose in life, associating purpose with achieving a goal, a vision. We can have several purposes: perhaps a certain career, a house with a garden, a family, a dog (thinking about my daughter – it might happen), or simply finding love.

These involve a process: To do something. To be somewhere. To search. To endeavour. To plan and execute. To be in love. To have a family. It all involves making judgements; always being focused on some point in the future. *What was wrong with that?* I rationalised. Everybody did it. Ask yourself if your life's purpose, disguised underneath all the other roles you play, is to be like others. The fact is that we are all trying to blend in. We are afraid to stand out. We are faithful neither to ourselves nor to others.

You need courage to stand out, to be known by who you really are. Not pretending. Not fearful of what others might think. You must have conviction, belief in yourself. You act accordingly (*karma*), to remain anchored. Martin Luther King reached the courageous milestone where he openly declared, "I'm not fearing any man," and thus found his spiritual freedom.

As I embarked on the journey of self-discovery, one of the teachings of the Sikh Gurus provided a simple message: "Have the courage to stand out from the crowd". It is OK to be different. But be faithful to the Guru's teachings by practising them. Be faithful to your Guru by being merciful, courageous, fearless. Love life as you would a wonderful play. I was ready to listen, learn and practise. I just needed a second chance.

I had confused ambition, dreams and goals as the purpose of life. If only I had paid attention to the teachings of the Guru. I had gone to the temple a couple of times every week for as long as I could remember, hearing rather than listening to the Guru's message about simple living. A message that was simple to understand and follow.

Don't confuse your dreams, ambitions and goals in life with your purpose, Guru ji says. You don't have to search for your purpose; you were born with it. There is nothing to search for, to look for or to do. Realise this. Let yourself be the experience. Recognise that everything that exists has the same purpose – to be life itself. The spirit pervading in all. Who would you hate then? Who would you judge? Always in bliss (*anand*), no matter the goal or ambition. To be yourself, the true self. That is your purpose. It is OK to have dreams and ambitions. Go for them, but with the wisdom of the Guru (*gian, naam, shabad*, the Word). Find your true purpose. For this you require humility, not timidity. For this I had to have a heart attack.

Humility and not timidity lets you look at yourself and others through a different lens. It changes how we think, what we expect and, as a result, how we behave. We then see open doors and opportunities where, previously, we looked but did not see or did not think to look. To be open to what is being given and not to reframe it, filter it or reinterpret it – to really accept it as it is given, with gratitude. This helps us understand the concept of surrender. Love delivers. It may not be what we want ... but it will be what we need.

Timidity is the ego in disguise. As Don Juan teaches Carlos Castaneda in *Journey to Ixtlan*:

> There is no time for timidity, simply because timidity makes you cling to something that exists only in your thoughts. It soothes you while everything is at a lull, but then the awesome, mysterious world will open its mouth for you, as it will open for every one of us, and then you will realize that your sure ways were not sure at all. Being timid prevents us from examining and exploiting our lot as men.

Similarly, Saint Augustine (354–430 AD), also known as Augustine of Hippo, an early Christian theologian and philosopher, gives the following advice based on a sermon in 1 John **4**:4–12: "Do you wish

7

to rise? Begin by descending. You plan a tower that will pierce the clouds? Lay first the foundation of humility."

Expanding on the sermon, Augustine said:

> See what we are insisting upon; that the deeds of men are only discerned by the root of charity. For many things may be done that have a good appearance, and yet proceed not from the root of charity. For thorns also have flowers: some actions truly seem rough, seem savage; how be it they are done for discipline at the bidding of charity. Once for all, then, a short precept is given you: Love, and do what you will: whether you hold your peace, through love hold your peace; whether you cry out, through love cry out; whether you correct, through love correct; whether you spare, through love do you spare: let the root of love be within, of this root can nothing spring but what is good.

These words would have a huge effect on my life after my recovery, as I embarked on a journey to work with those who needed a helping hand – working with farmers and their families in Africa, beautiful people with a tenacity and resilience I have not seen elsewhere. And they have so little. But I am getting carried away – more about this phase of my life later. Let us focus on the present.

Here I am, in 2017, living an active, happy life and grateful for my continued learning – self-discovery made possible through a fresh conviction that I will always be looked after as long as I allow myself to give and receive love and compassion. As the Sikh *shabad* says: *"jo mange thakhar apnay tay, soi soi deway"* ("Love gives what you honestly ask of it"). "This world is like a mountain," says Shams-i-Tabrīzī, an Iranian Sunni Muslim who is credited as the spiritual instructor of Rumi. "Your echo depends on you. If you scream good things, the world will give it back. If you scream bad things, the world will give it back. Even if someone speaks badly about you, speak well about him. Change your heart to change the world." Similarly, in Matthew 7:7–8 it is stated: "Ask, and it shall be given you; seek, and ye shall find; knock, and it shall be opened unto you: For every one that asketh receiveth; and he that seeketh findeth; and to him that knocketh it shall be opened."

But there is a condition. You have to surrender, let go of all that you know, to something that is all-powerful, to something that is within you and has always been there, never changing, never judging.

Well, I had to be forced to be helpless, lying in hospital, to surrender and let go of the constant bombardment of thoughts about the past, the present and the future, over which I thought I had control. The process of being forced to let go was tortuous and traumatic, but I moved away from my imagined authority and supremacy over how life works. Things, or my perception of them, had changed. This was a blessing because this change led to the achievement of bigger and better things for me.

Looking at death in the face turns you into a philosopher. It makes you fearless (*nirbhau, nirvair*). You learn to take each breath with gratitude and make the best of this gift of life. Isn't this another way of saying live in the moment? Let go of all our baggage. Be free and light.

I took a step towards living joyfully with and beside people, rather than behaving as if I was special, and learning from the Sikh *shabad*, "*Aaagey sukh meray mita, pachay anand prabh kita*" ("Live in the present moment as the awareness and be in constant bliss").

The Sikh Gurus have a simple message for all mankind: Your light is part of the universal light. You are joined to this. *Apna mool pechan* – "recognise this". Recognise your worth; recognise yourself; recognise yourself as the eternal light/energy. Grace (*gurprasad*) is the conduit between your finite (conditioned) self and what more you can experience and become – your infinite self. Others who walked the path have observed and declared the same.

And we are all the same *mool*. The lamps are different, says Rumi, but the light is the same. One matter, one energy, one light, one light-mind, endlessly emanating all things.

As Lao Tzu says in the *Tao Te Ching*:

> My teachings are easy to understand and easy to put into practice. Yet your intellect will never grasp them, and if you try to practise them, you will fail. My teachings are older than

the world. How can you grasp their meaning? If you want to know me, look inside your heart.

He further expresses it in this beautiful poem:

Since before time and space were, the Tao is.
It is beyond is and is not.
How do I know this is true?
I look inside myself and see.

This is all serious stuff, you might think. A bit ethereal. So here is an anecdote to help you along.

It was the month of Ramadhan, and followers of Islam were fasting. However, a few young disciples of Bulleh Shah (1680–1757), a Sufi spiritual teacher and philosopher, were caught eating carrots by the local police of the same faith.

"Why are you eating and not fasting?" they demanded to know, after a few slaps.

"Our *Murshad* [teacher] Bulleh Shah said it was OK," they replied.

"Where is he now?" the police demanded to know.

"Inside this cave, praying," they answered, sobbing.

When confronted by the police and upon being asked who he was, Bulleh Shah replied, "I have no idea who I am, I am still looking".

Thinking him to be a madman, the police spared him the slaps.

Let us not try to make sense of everything in life. Not knowing all the answers is not to be a failure. Leave some mystery in your lives; it makes life unpredictable. You don't have to carry out a risk assessment on life. Be "mad". Just live life, with no smokescreens.

We have created smokescreens, and lost our anchor through culture, religion, education, caste, sex, experiences, society, etc. We are conditioned, which isolates us from each other. Clear the smoke to re-anchor yourself and then this light or love connection, which has always been inside you, becomes the guide again.

I present this book to you as a service so that we can share learning. We are not alone. We only have to learn how to ask for the help we need. For me, this help came and continues to come through a commitment to what the Sikh Gurus preached as *sangat* (congregation), *sewa* (selfless service and living), *ardhas* (prayer), *simran* (constant practice of compassion, humility), *anand* (bliss) and *dharma* (the practice of humanity, beyond the boundaries of religion).

This book attempts to shine a light on the presence of these gifts around us all the time. In fact, what is around us is also within us. We are part of that unbroken thread of giving and receiving with compassion. Don't take it too seriously. Enjoy it and make your own sense of it. We all tread different paths, but the destination is the same. With this in mind, the book attempts to bring in teachings from different faiths, philosophers and saints. The book is a service to all the people who have crossed my path – and to those who will. It is a service to you, the reader. Yes, I am sorry you had to pay for it. You know the whole shebang about costs and all that.

Chapter 1 is about the *sangat* within which we exist. We do not live in isolation. Poets, philosophers and psychologists have highlighted this at length. It is more than not being an island, or interacting with like-minded souls. Chapter 1 makes visible the *sangat* who are with us daily on our journey and who cross our path on different timescales and for different purposes. *Sadh sangat* lifts you with love. It is why I am still here, writing this.

Chapter 2 is about *sewa* – unconditional service to all. A feeling of being overcome by the fact that we are part of a connected existence compels us to play our part in supporting the collective well-being. *"Harkasewak, so harjeha"* ("A servant of love embodies love") (*SGGS*). What does service do to how we relate to other people? What realisation brings us this urge to serve? What can be the effect of this – physically, emotionally and socially? *Sewa* makes us face people. You say we are equal? Show me. That is why *sewa* is not easy. We turn intention with ego into action with humility.

Chapter 3 is about *ardhas* (prayer). We don't have to be religious to say a prayer. Just speak to the universe. It's all around us, and within us. It may feel like talking to yourself. It can be, but, with the right intention and with no expectation, we are not waiting to receive anything in particular. We are open to accepting whatever happens (or is offered). Something happens when you let go of expectations and pray. You stop resisting. You are seeking blessings, to be in the embrace of your beloved, grace (*gurprasad*). There is nothing to resist against. The imagined cage from which we want release is of our own making. It dissolves when we are tuned into the God in all of us. "To thine own self be true." Then, we stop trying to run with the wind. Instead, our actions are guided by what is of meaningful consequence in our lives. By the grace of God, drop by drop, we are moved on to new realisations.

Chapter 4 is about *jap* (meditation) and *simran* (the practice of the Guru's teachings). Through this we can create a "sacred space" that can help us move beyond the constant thoughts and empty self-talk in our heads and begin to think more freely and meaningfully. While the practice of *jap* quietens the mind, *simran* reflects and practises the qualities attributed to God (*Waheguru*), such as unconditional love, compassion, courage, fearlessness and forgiveness. We are led to see that we have these qualities in us already. How can we live and grow guided by this, our "honest" nature? Not the one that we show to others, or wish for, or claim to be, but the human being we see when we face ourselves honestly. The Guru's *shabad* "*Har ka simran sabh te ucha*" reminds us to "meditate upon the love inside and between us" because it comes from and leads to everything else.

Chapter 5 is about *anand* (bliss). Sometimes I just feel I am living in an embrace of love; I am not worried about what comes next. I know I will be led to what I need – a thought shared by Saint Francis: "We do not need to struggle. We will be given, we should not worry." The moments in my life are beginning not to distract me by making me think of what was or could be. The moments themselves sometimes feel like gifts. I try to surrender to them … and then my relationship with the people and events in my life changes … from expectation to gratitude. "If the only prayer you say in your life is 'thank you,' that would suffice," observes Eckhart Tolle, a spiritual teacher and author born in Germany and educated in the United Kingdom. At the age of 29, a profound inner transformation radically changed the course of his life. He is the author of the best-selling *The Power of Now: A Guide to Spiritual Enlightenment*, and *A New Earth: Awakening to Your Life's Purpose*, regarded as two of the most influential spiritual books of our time. No wonder the comedian Jim Carrey once remarked, "I would do anything to be anywhere in the vicinity of Eckhart Tolle".

Chapter 6 is about "living as the *mool*," the spirit. For me, this is about two important truths. Truth number one is to take responsibility for everything that happens to us in every moment of life. This is clearly expressed by the Sikh Gurus in the shabad *"Aapae beej apae hee khaahu Nanak hukamee aavahu jaahu"* ("What I sow is what I reap. Accept this law of life."). The second truth is that I can change what happens to my life. *Sangat, sewa* and *simran* can help. The intention is set by the *ardhas*. Together, these keys tune you into what you really want to do and become. They enable you to live guided by your courage and compassion – the saint-soldier in you – rather than by the ever-changing winds that blow in our daily lives. As Rumi said, "I looked in temples, churches and mosques. But I found the Divine within my heart."

Chapter 7 is about the Sikhs and their Gurus. This chapter provides an overview of Sikh teachings, and is aimed at readers to whom they might not be very clear.

Chapter 8 is about learning. How and what we learn is important. But more important than the gathering of knowledge is what we do with it – our practice of it. The learning that comes from practice has to help one take further steps towards discovering one's *mool*. It is not how much you know but what you do with that knowledge that is important. Practise, practise is the message – don't just be a hunter-gatherer. We have limited time. You can be called back by your maker without a moment's notice. Change comes slowly, like enlightenment.

Please forgive any shortcomings and accept this writing as you would from your *sewak*, a servant of the Guru.

RECOGNISE YOUR LIGHT WITHIN - **APNA MOOL PECHAN**

"Waheguru Ji Ka Khalsa Waheguru Ji Ki Fateh."

A phrase used by Sikhs as a greeting and farewell – a simple reminder that the soul is at the centre of all creation and that recognition of this truth is your victory. Victory of the Guru. Victory of the Creator.

Chapter 1

Sangat – Re-anchor to say, "Thank you, I met you again today"

Nanak Sikh Dhaee Man Preetham Saadhasang Bhram Jaalae

"Nanak gives this advice: O dear mind, in the *Saadh-Sangat*, burn away your doubts." (*SGGS*)

All that was "home" for me and gave me the experience of "my life" was taken from me. For a short time, I felt as if I belonged nowhere. Two thoughts to share. Firstly, we live in the comfort of people and environments we do not fully notice, until we lose them. Then we realise that what was most comforting about life was what we noticed least. That is not, in itself, a shortcoming. It is because those aspects are too close to us to see. We feel them by their presence and absence.

All I wanted to do, as I recovered from the heart attack, was to stand on the corner of Southall Broadway and feel the energy of people of all ages and backgrounds walking up and down this very busy part of west London. I just wanted to take in the amalgamation of smells drifting out from the numerous Indian restaurants that line both sides of the Broadway. I wanted to listen to the music coming from the stalls selling CDs of religious and cultural music; and taste the *jalebis* (a sweet fried savoury) and *cholay bhaturay* (spiced chick peas and traditional fried bread) from the stalls. I just wanted to feel part of the wonderful flow of life again. Fried or not. Don't listen to everything the doctor says. (Just kidding.).

I couldn't express it better than Rumi, who said: "I learned that every mortal will taste death, but only some will taste life". He didn't mean it in the literal sense, I am sure. He probably meant what I felt.

Being alive meant being able to appreciate the five senses we take for granted – to be able to savour every experience in life.

To experience the miracle of life. An unfolding of life and awareness. Discovering that man is the soul and has a body. Being the experience itself. Never judging. Never affected. No duality – duality being the perception of "me" (the self) as being separate from the "other" (object). The spirit never getting old or sick, or dying.

Then there is the miracle of birth. One sperm in millions fertilises an egg. Carried and looked after in the womb for nine months. Born into a world of endless wonder and possibility. Developing individuality, emotions and thoughts. An emotional body and a mental one. Believing man *is* a body and *has* a soul. The body has perceptions. The body has experiences – good and bad.

I had been busy living as the body, always looking after its comforts. Never realising that it could collapse and cease to exist in a second, in a moment. I had heard the Guru's message countless times: "You are the spirit. That is the miracle of life," he kept reminding me, but, as usual, I had not been listening or paying attention. I had become too attached to my role-playing, such as husband, provider, father master manipulator. Our five senses – sight, hearing, touch, taste and smell – feed information to the mind. They are focused outwards. They feed into the mind. They give rise to perceptions. We make decisions based on perceptions – an inner voice that tells us what is right and what is wrong. Common sense making judgements about situations. Our perceptions change with changing information. The mind is always busy trying to keep up. Judging, criticising and being selfish. Never in one place. Living in the past, present and future. It's me versus the rest of the world. Living a self-centred life.

While, all along, Guru ji had wanted to guide me back to my being-ness. To have "one" identity. A fixed point (*saachaa naam maeraa aadhhaaro*), from where I could play, all the other roles. I needed my Guru's help, but first I had to learn how to approach him.

I found out that my Guru had a very simple rule and that was to leave my mind, with all its complexities and cleverness, on the "rack" outside his door. That is how I had to bow, in reverence. When

I learnt to do this and be with my Guru, the Guru himself began making changes in me. He washed out all that I had accumulated over the years and began to fill me with his love.

There is another way of living, I was to realise. To learn to use my five senses (*indriyas*) as spiritual instruments, focused inwards. The Guru and *sangat* provides the fountain of spiritual knowledge. To use my senses through meditation, selfless service and prayer to awaken an inner awareness. To see, feel, touch, taste and smell my oneness with all that exists. No separation. To feel deep down that life happens. To quieten the mind (*maan*). No perceptions - just oneness.

This gives rise to the second question: What do we become attached to? What is the thread of attachment? (Clue: It is not jalebis!) Standing in a place that feels like home, surrounded by people I do not know. What does that represent? What am I doing, and why? Perhaps John Green, author of *The Fault in Our Stars* (2012), had the answer when he said, "Grief does not change you, it reveals you". The title is inspired by Act 1, Scene 2 of Shakespeare's *Julius Caesar*, in which the nobleman Cassius says to Brutus: "The fault, dear Brutus, is not in our stars, but in ourselves, that we are underlings". Green's story is narrated by a 16-year-old cancer patient who, forced by her parents to attend a support group, meets and falls in love with 17-year-old amputee.

I realised that I had spent my life mostly in my own company, oblivious of everything around me, like a train with brake failure, rushing down a steep hill, heading for certain oblivion. I had become used to this rush to nowhere and, in the process, forming habits that reinforced and justified this mentality. "Curious things, habits," wrote the novelist Agatha Christie (1890–1976); "people themselves never knew they had them."

In the Sikh *dharma*, *sadh sangat* is a term with its origin in the Sanskrit word "*sangh*", meaning company, fellowship and association with those who are on a spiritual path. At the end of the Sikh prayer (*ardhas*), there is a plea to God (you can use your own interpretation of this greater power) that goes like this: "*Sae-ee piaarae maelo jinhaan' miliaan' Taeraa Naam chitt aavae. Nanak Naam charh'dee kalaa, T'arae bhaanae sarbatt daa bhalaa.*" (usually

17

translated as "Grant me the company of those who may help keep Your name fresh in our hearts. Through Satguru Nanak, may Your name be exalted and may all of mankind prosper according to your Will.")

The *sadh sangat*, congregation, the *sangha*, the *minyan* and the *halka* offer spiritual brotherhood and sisterhood within the context of life in the greater community. The group serves as a container for energies and as a reminder of the sacred.

I feel it is more than that. The whole is bigger than the sum of its parts. To me, it is a plea to the universe to grace me with a life that keeps me in the realisation that I am always surrounded by love – unconditional love that helps everybody live unafraid and with humanity. I was about to discover this – but through an event that would jolt me out of a deep slumber that had been my life before.

In the early hours of a hot Monday morning in June 1996, I was rushed to hospital following a massive heart attack. It is funny how one event out of countless others in our lives can turn your life upside down. That moment came to me with the stark realisation that I had (nearly) run out of time without a moment's notice. (As I wrote this last sentence, I smiled: a life-changing event without a moment's notice! Wow! How long is a moment? A second? A millisecond? As long as a thought? How long is a thought?).

For me – and, believe me, this is based on first-hand experience – a moment can be as short as the flick of a switch. And you cannot do anything to stop it being flicked. My switch somehow got stuck, and I was lucky to have survived; and that gave me the space to shine a spotlight on my life. The shocking realisation of the unpredictability of life; the false perceptions of permanence on which plans and dreams are built; the foolish illusion of the power of control over others; the baseless assumptions about happiness and contentment – all stood out starkly under the spotlight. It wasn't a pretty picture, and my whole approach to life shook to its very foundations.

The doctor in charge recommended that I have a clot-busting injection to prevent further damage, but warned that the drug might cause internal bleeding and damage other organs.

I hesitated, but an elderly nurse attending another patient in the next cubicle came over, took my hand and said, "Please have the injection. You are young and it can save your life." Something about her earnest manner convinced me to have the injection. It did indeed save my life. I think about that nurse often. Yes, good doctors and nurses have that universal vision to notice and to act wherever they can help; they work beyond labels and job titles. But why did she come over to me from her own patient, and give that specific advice? Compassion as medicine. Compassion as purpose. A cornerstone for anybody concerned with reducing suffering.

It is certainly not self-centredness and self-absorption. We see these as unappealing personality traits in a friend, colleague or partner. We feel that both self-centred and self-absorbed people are more concerned with their image and materialistic things. They don't bother to take the time to understand another person's point of view or feelings. Now I had to look at myself with the same critical eye.

Much later, as I reflected on this, a number of questions arose in my mind. Do we maintain a sense of compassion and understanding towards others? Do we complain or whine all the time, no matter what? Experiencing the compassion and kindness of strangers made me ashamed of myself. I had to stop being needy. Stop contracting myself, limiting myself. Stop being self-centred and self-absorbed.

While in intensive care, I was heavily medicated at first. As the staff eased up on the medicine, I felt myself regaining my clarity of sight and thought. As I became more aware of what I was going through, fear gripped me in spasms, with a defiant resilience in between. The struggle was fierce. Sometimes I lost heart, but I did not feel I was losing faith.

Then, one morning, I was rendered motionless. I suddenly saw what only I could see. I saw three figures watching over me – clear as daylight, and dressed as traditional Sikh warriors, the Khalsa. They stood tall and majestic in the doorway, not speaking, just watching. I have always believed in God's infinite love and compassion. I saw what I saw. No dissection, no unpacking, a no-brainer. For me, it was a sign that all would be well. Without a moment's hesitation, I felt a physical and spiritual lift from their presence and vowed to fight for my life. It is difficult to capture the significance of this moment, but the neurologist, naturalist and writer Oliver Sacks (1933–2015) comes close:

> There are moments, and it is only a matter of five or six seconds, when you feel the presence of the eternal harmony … a terrible thing is the frightful clearness with which it manifests itself and the rapture with which it fills you. If this state were to last more than five seconds, the soul could not endure it and would have to disappear. During these five seconds I live a whole human existence, and for that I would give my whole life and not think that I was paying too dearly. (Oliver Sacks, *The Man Who Mistook His Wife for a Hat and Other Clinical Tales*)

The ebb and flow of my thoughts and emotions calmed down. I felt drained and beaten to the ground. Yet, in amongst this despairing experience, I felt a small part of me stand firm. I clung to this: my base, my stability, and the part of me that seemed to be untouchable by my collapse. I could not speak about it. Enigmatic and a source of comfort, I am reminded of Kahlil Gibran saying, "In the depth of my soul there is a wordless song".

As I was wheeled back into my room after an angiogram and angioplasty, I found my wife, distraught and worn out by her own suffering. A young doctor had advised her to get her affairs in order. The odds on my survival were not good. Even if I did survive, they said, my life would be challenging.

She looked at me pleadingly and made me promise I would pull through. She had lost her father when she was a little girl and had experienced the trauma and challenges of her mother being a single parent. I made the promise with conviction. This storm in our lives would pass. We seemed to strengthen each other's resolve.

We are responsible for those to whom we are connected. I could feel her sense of impending loss, but it was overshadowed by the love I saw as I lay in my hospital bed. I couldn't bear to see her this way. I felt responsible for it. I wanted to use that little strength in me to stop her suffering. When I agreed to participate in a new drugs trial and started taking the new medication, I began to feel less like a zombie and more like my old self. To my surprise, I had been taking placebos. Initially confused, I remembered that I also had the loving embrace of my wife and family. I remembered how good it felt to feel their love. Calm breathing, calm mind and a feeling of the body sinking into rest and comfort. Compassion as medicine. It cannot be ignored.

I was being nurtured by strangers and my wife. Perhaps the Tao is the *sangat* that helps you shed all your beliefs about your infallibility and opens your eyes to true, unconditional love. And to the discovery of the *mool* that each of us really is once the layers of years of conditioning have been stripped away to just being and living as the spirit.

What contribution does a strong spirit, care, love and compassion make to recovery? I am not recommending that you stop taking your medication. I am simply suggesting that external events and how we experience them within can create the right physical and chemical environment for our bodies and medicines to work together in the healing process. This is why one of the best medical treatments is to strengthen the immune system, our defence against disease and sickness. The body is very good at healing itself – given the chance.

We are a part of the whole, the *mool* within us and the *sangat*. As Albert Einstein said:

> A human being is a part of the whole called by us the "universe", a part limited in time and space. He experiences himself, his thoughts and feeling as something separated from the rest – a kind of optical delusion of his consciousness. This delusion is a kind of prison for us, restricting us to our personal desires and to affection for a few persons nearest to us. Our task must be to free ourselves from this prison by widening our circles of compassion to embrace all living creatures and the whole of nature in its beauty.

It was at a Sikh temple that I fell in love for the first time. I was 16. It was mostly one-way; I loved, she ignored. I was a small-town boy and she a city girl. I tried to impress with my *tabla*-playing skills. She had heard better.

A year later, she got married. I was heartbroken, but learnt something amazing about myself. I was immersed in this incredible feeling of surrender and unconditional love, and it did not matter that it was not reciprocated. I just felt a powerful desire to feel and give, without expectation. I just appreciated my ability to experience it all. She was never mine. If something is right for you, you receive it. If not, perhaps it is not meant for you. Or maybe later and not right now.

My wife was waiting for me, and I for her – to save my life. I came as soon as I could. I got married in 1979 to Gursharan. I was 24 and she 22. As we got into the car to depart from her home, I earnestly promised her grandfather that I would look after her. Little did I know that it would be the other way round! My wife took the brunt of everything I went through, and never complained. I honestly do not know how she is wired. Always calm, composed, smiling and soldiering on. Always happy, without any elaborate professing of what that means, she just makes the most of the here and now.

She always says, "I am here for you". She was. And she is. I remembered the song lyrics, "If tomorrow never comes, would she know how much I loved her?". We are not told often enough that we are loved. Nor do we tell others that we love them. My trauma has made me more loving, rather than hardening me and making me fearful. I always was loving, but realised that I did not show it enough. Now I do – and it feels so natural.

When you find the love of your life (and it may even be one-sided), what is the condition of your mind, your heart? Where do all the praises you sing for the "one" arise from? Aren't they rooted in a deeper place within you that cannot be pinpointed? Doesn't this love come from a deep place within that feels lost and incomplete without the "one"?

When this happens, the only way we remember the "one" is through constant praise. We cannot stop repeating "I love this and I love that about you". We are eager to share this praise with others, too. We want to share every moment and experience with the special one. These praises are not reasoned out or justified by some thinking process – they just *are*. They are your bare self, stripped of every pretence or world-view. But there is always a fear of not being loved the same way, or of losing it. It happens.

I had found love that is always present, overwhelming, engulfing. Love that is not based on fear. Never being unsure of being loved back. Love that keeps you whole in every moment. Supporting you. Making you confident and creative. Always with the beloved. Never alone.

I am only here because of others. I want to give back and immerse myself in our connected living. Maybe Karl Jung was right when he said that we are not what has happened to us as human beings; we are what we choose to become. George Kelly, an American psychologist, echoed this when he spoke about how we construe, or make meaning of, events in our lives: "No person needs to be a victim of his or her own biography," he said.

Our lives should not be about fear and our search for protection and support. Fear can dominate our thinking and our actions, which in itself can stop us from seeing what protection and support we already have. It has brought us here … and it will not leave us.

We all live in constant fear. It is imagined because of how we perceive things as they are now or as they may happen, or past events. Mainly our fear is that life may not go the way we wish. What we want to happen may not happen. That is our fear. Fear always involves the other; if somebody can take something away from you, it destroys our security. This includes death and illness, work, relationships – they are all the "other".

Feel the company of *sangat*, be the *sangat*. We are all connected and there for each other. Everything outside is inside too. If not, how would you recognise it? Meet the universe, meet yourself. When there is no "other", what is there to fear? Accept what happens and find the good in it. Break the downward spiral of pessimism and imagining that one event that was not what you wanted leads to disaster and catastrophe. It does not.

Sangat protects you by guiding and nurturing you. *Sewa* (selfless service) protects you by giving you the experience of living in the *sangat*. *Simran*, the constant practice of compassion and forgiveness, reminds you of what truly connects you. You are not alone. You have come far. There is nothing to be afraid of.

Similar sentiments were expressed by Shams-i-Tabrīzī, Rumi's teacher. He said: "We are living as part of a loving community who live by sharing love and showing it … there are no strangers. Only people we know, and others we do not know yet." He continued:

> The universe is a complete unique entity. Everything and everyone is bound together with some invisible strings. Do not break anyone's heart; do not look down on [those] weaker than you. One's sorrow at the other side of the world can make the entire world suffer; one's happiness can make the entire world smile.

A Sikh *shabad* says, "*Sab ko meet hum apen keena. Hum sabna ke sajan.*" ("I consider everybody I meet my friends and compatriots, and in return I am also their friend and compatriot.").

To me, this is the true meaning of *sangat* – recognising and acknowledging that a single energy force exists within all of creation, without judgement, without labelling. Every moment of your life is the culmination of not only all your own efforts and hard work, but also of the efforts of many souls and incidents that have touched your path. Enjoy and embrace the discovery of that interconnectedness.

Oliver Sacks provides a wonderful analogy of this when discussing the brain:

> The brain is more than an assemblage of autonomous modules, each crucial for a specific mental function. Every one of these functionally specialized areas must interact with dozens or hundreds of others, their total integration creating something like a vastly complicated orchestra with thousands of instruments, an orchestra that conducts itself, with an ever-changing score and repertoire.

Look and see what is happening around us. It can be difficult to see other than what we want to see. Accept what happens as what is happening. Then decide what you want to do and, for now, what you are able to do. These realisations drove my deep desire to stand on the pavements of Southall Broadway. Feel the beating life of the *sangat* within and around me. No separation, just going back home. My comfort is where I belong, in the embrace of *sangat*. Their embrace has brought me so far. I know I am in safe hands.

To remain compassionate with ourselves, so that we may nurture our aspirations. Not succumbing to catastrophising but letting ourselves shine and grow. This requires discipline, awareness, trust, and a strong personal vision for wanting the very best for ourselves and for others. Holding close that connection that tells us that one person's fall weakens us all. This is a part of what *sangat* contributes to everyone's success.

At any time, there are people who reflect this commitment and discipline to the well-being of everybody. "*Sarbhat da bhalla*" is the Sikh prayer that asks for the well-being of all. There are others who are distracted and have yet to grow that far. All of them are *sangat*. Maybe *sangat* is all of life. Always present, listening to you and ready to help if only you will be open and say "yes" to the moment. This can be obstructed when we are overwhelmed by feelings of resentment, fear for our own safety and well-being, and a disregard for others' well-being.

We can be weakened by feelings of isolation from the experience of *sangat*. Sometimes the scars of living, which we all carry, subdue our true selves. Our scars heal at different rates and leave behind a legacy of sometimes debilitating memories and emotions. *Sangat* shows you that the scars have come and gone and helps you to let go. It shows you a constant flow of acts of bravery, courage, conviction and discipline. Through *sangat* you see possibilities for your own life – not a purpose for our lives, but possibilities. Possibilities of expression.

I had thought I had found my purpose in life. I had associated purpose with achieving a goal, a vision. And I had several "purposes". A business that was the envy of others, a cut above the rest. A colonial-style bungalow with a small stream, in the woods. A family and finding love. And I wanted a particular kind of dog. A lazy dog, with sad but mischievous eyes, who expected to be served. To be the master. A dog that would bark if there was a suspicious sound but not bother to go and check. A dog who would be fat and lazy, but cute, always there, in the same place, with the only detectable sign of life being the occasional twitching of its ears.

Having a purpose involved a process. To do something. To be somewhere. To search. To endeavour. To plan and execute. To be in love. To have a family. It involved making judgements. Always being focused on some point in the future – not living and appreciating the experiences of the moment.

Sangat reminds us not to confuse these with our true purpose. You don't have to search for your purpose. You were born with it. There is nothing to search for. To look for. To do. Just realise it. Let yourself become the experience. Recognising that all that exists has the same purpose: to be life itself. The spirit pervading in all. Who would you hate then? Who would you judge? Always in a state of bliss (*anand*), no matter the goal or ambition. To be yourself, the true self. That is your purpose. The rest are just goals for which you are striving. Have ambitions. Go for them, but with the wisdom of the Guru (*gian, naam, shabad*). Find your true purpose. And *sangat* reminds you of this.

"Accept everything just the way it is," wrote Miyamoto Musashi in his composition *Dokkodo (The Way of Walking Alone)*. Very simply, I learnt to relax in the company of *sangat,* safe in the knowledge that I am taken care of. The world looks different when viewed from a relaxed mind and body. You can respond so much more freely and with conviction. There are no layers of memories and residual emotions obscuring what you are truly observing, or what you really want to do. If you know what you really want to do, you can do it.

Surrendering, so that we are open to possibilities and to being guided by what is meaningful, is not easy. Yet we need this in all parts of our lives. Henry Miller said in *The Wisdom of the Heart*:

> To relax is, of course, the first thing a dancer has to learn. It
> is also the first thing a patient has to learn when he confronts
> the analyst. It is the first thing any one has to learn in order to

live. It is extremely difficult, because it means surrender, full surrender.

Full surrender meant acknowledging and accepting unconditionally, Guru ji, as my mentor, guide and companion. In return, he guided me onto a journey that is now fluid and full of serendipity and surprise. Every moment and every breath is new and fresh.

Sangat guided me to let go, bit by bit, my constant judgements, jealousy, anger and attachments to material things. This in turn, created a space within me, that quickly filled with boundless love. Accepting life as it comes to me, in the full knowledge and trust that my Guru knows what is best for me. In the company of the sangat, we learn to become a fakir, a "behang" (*rahay behangam katayna jahi*), with no worries and demands.

Feel the company of *sangat*, be the *sangat*. Use it as a mirror. Everything outside is inside too. If not, how would you recognise it? Shed all your doubts about the infinite that you are. Meet the universe – meet yourself.

As I recovered, I began to recognise and experience the love of strangers and friends who crossed my path, and it struck me quite clearly that you are always being provided by the universe with people and events that take you closer to recognising your *mool*. Jeff Warner, a performer/interpreter of traditional music, says, "We are not put on this earth for ourselves, but are placed here for each other. If you are there always for others, then in time of need, someone will be there for you."

All you need to do is be like an empty vessel with its opening facing upwards so that grace, which is pouring on all creation at all times, can come in and fill it. My trouble was that conceit had weighted my pot and it had toppled upside down. It took a heart attack, a near-death experience, to flip it the right way up and *sangat* to begin emptying it slowly. *Sewa* and *ardhas* completed this emptying, and *grace* slowly began to fill it. What is grace but bliss, or *anand* as the Sikh Gurus called it?

The following *shabad* provides guidance on *sangat*: "*Sachi baisak tina sang jin sang japiai nao. Tin Sang sang na kichai Nanak jina*

27

apna suao." ("True is the society of those in whose company thy name is meditated upon. Nanak, associate not with those who have their own self-interest.") (*SGGS*)

Get to know yourself (*sant kirpa tay andin jaag*). Your companion is within you – only you have chosen to ignore him. A companion that has humility, and is never judging, always forgiving and compassionate. Always there with you, for you. Surrender to this truth. You are that companion. Be that, stay there. Confident, fearless and loving. Let go of the control of the mind. Trees show how lovely it is to let dead leaves go. Accept life as it comes to you (*hukam*). The *sangat* is as much within you as around you. Be the *sangat*.

Chapter 2

Sewa – Unconditional and selfless service of the sangat

Anik Bhaanth Kar Sewa Kareeai. Jeeo Praan Dhhan Aagai
Dhhareeai
"*Sewa* is of many types, and performed different ways.
Serve God dedicating your Soul, your breath of life and your
wealth." (*SGGS*)

I grew up in Thika, a small town in Kenya, about 45 kilometres
north-east of central Nairobi. The Asian community, comprising
Hindus, Sikhs and Muslims, was close-knit, living like one big
family, and everyone knew everyone else. All festivals and special
occasions were celebrated jointly and people trusted each other
and helped one another to get ahead in whatever they were doing.
Any conflict was quickly resolved, and the community sat together
to figure out how best to get the children educated and to explore
new opportunities.

Any child found wanting in his or her behaviour could be
reprimanded by anybody, no questions asked. This form of collective
responsibility really worked and, for the most part, we trod a straight
path. Don't get me wrong; we did get into a lot of mischief, but
we just had to be careful. That actually became the fun part – not
getting caught. But it was all innocent fun.

From very early in primary school, teachers made us learn and
practise values reflected in proverbs that built good behaviour.
These proverbs still play an important part in my daily life. Sadly,
I notice that these character-building proverbs are no longer taught
in schools. I once attended a presentation that included data from a

survey showing that if you asked people what was the most useful thing they had learnt recently, they would say facts and information. If you asked them what was the best thing they had *ever* learnt, maxims or guidance about how to live came out on top.

Classics amongst what we were taught included "Two wrongs don't make a right". We learnt about the futility of revenge. "No man is an island" taught us about friendship, interdependence and responsibility for each other. "People who live in glass houses should not throw stones" taught us about the dangers of hypocrisy, and the importance of humility and compassion. Once you recognise that your relationship with somebody is not defined by age or job titles, you see one *sangat* with an unconditional responsibility for each other's lives. This unconditional responsibility of selfless service is *sewa*.

We learnt very early what it meant to be a part of a community. To do *sewa*.

Sewa is unconditional and selfless service of the *sangat*. In the Sikh faith, *sewa* takes many forms. On one level, it includes cleaning the *sangat*'s shoes at the *gurdwara*, cleaning utensils of the *sangat*, cooking and serving food in the *langar* (communal kitchen), carrying out other cleaning duties around the temple, or *kirtan* (narrating) and *chaur sahib* (fanning) of the Guru Granth Sahib. On another, it involves feeding and clothing the poor, providing support and resources to the disadvantaged, standing up to injustices suffered by those without a voice, providing access to education or simply making available the time to speak and listen to the lonely.

In his book *Capitalism: As if the World Matters*, the environmentalist and writer Jonathon Porritt relates community to sustainability by highlighting similar values: "… the core values that underpin sustainable development – interdependence, empathy, equity, personal responsibility and intergenerational justice – are the only foundation upon which any viable vision of a better world can possibly be constructed".

Growing up in Kenya, temples felt more like caring community centres. Everybody – Sikh, Hindu and Muslim – went and enjoyed the interactions, sharing of food, a lot of storytelling, catching up and being exposed to religious teachings. It was never a serious affair and there was no drumming-in of religious messages. There was a general unspoken consensus that all were equal, regardless of religious labels. Everybody attended everybody else's functions and carried out *sewa*.

The experience of *sewa* allows a different expression – pure love and compassion. Nothing is expected in return because a service to one is a service to all. If you allow it, it is also a service to the self. The fog finally lifts, drifting away far into the distance. Vigilance is required to balance intentions and emotions. We tend to admire our work after we have done it. Fine, but do not let that become the intention; this is to bow your head to the *sangat*, and offer the best of yourself. The road to hell is paved with good intentions that have become insincere or self-obsessed.

I had tried for a long time to force change within myself. For instance, I would say: from this point forward, whatever happens, I am not going to get angry. Of course, that did not last long, because years of conditioning said otherwise. And as soon as I lost my temper, I would feel more unworthy. Until, that is, I discovered, with the Guru's blessings, the true nature and meaning of *sewa* and the spirit within. I quickly realised that the emptying process was being accelerated by serving the *sangat* and that a void, a space within myself, was being created – a space where my own self-created self-identity was ceasing to exist.

In this way, *sewa* strips away, layer by layer, years of conditioning, and lays bare your true essence. Arrogance turns into humility, anger into compassion, hate into love, attachment into freedom, and lust into respect.

Aap guvaae sevaa kurae thaa kishh paaeae maan. ("But if he eliminates his self-conceit and then performs service, he will be honoured.") (*SGGS*)

Change comes through a gentle transformation that stays embedded in oneself. It is not forced from the outside, by the mind, but comes easily from within because, deep down, that is what we have always

31

been (Siri Mooji). The Greek philosopher Aristotle (384–322 BC) put it quite aptly: "Men acquire a particular quality by constantly acting a particular way … you become just by performing just actions, temperate by performing temperate actions, brave by performing brave actions."

My father had deep roots in the local community, always eager to develop new ideas in advancing the cultural and religious teachings of the Sikh Gurus. He was a keen musician and a harmonium (small organ) was by his side whenever he had some free time. He would always play and sing in the living room after his lunch and during the evening. At the weekend, he would sing a *shabad* or two at the local Sikh temple.

He encouraged me to learn to play the *tabla* – Indian percussion drums – a talent I still have and practise, rather proudly. Playing the *tabla* probably resulted in my developing a deep-rooted love of music, including a deeper connection with the Sikh Gurus as the Sikh Holy Scriptures, written in classical prose, are put to music as *ragas*.

I am blessed to have this skill because this is a *sewa* still carried out at the local *gurdwara*, serving the *sangat*. I cannot really say what impact this *sewa* has on the *sangat*. They come to listen and gain something from the *gurdwara*, and that is their journey. I gain by playing, they by listening. Certainly, while carrying out this *sewa*, I lose myself. I feel in a place of wondrous connected respect and humility. Just to visit this place inside me reminds me of what is deeper inside me, and feels more like ME than much else that I do.

My mother is a strong-minded and independent person. Like my father, she did not have any education, and had to leave her parents when she got married at a very young age. She lives her life with no expectations, actively participating in events celebrated by the local community in the true spirit of *sewa*. Life needs to be lived through service, she always says. She has always been adventurous in her outlook on life, something that can only come from a naïve sense that, no matter what, things will be OK. Things always work out – and they do.

She was responsible for the well-being of us all. In those days, the father figure commanded a certain respect, involving a relationship that had clear boundaries that could not be crossed. This included keeping a respectful distance, not showing rude behaviour, being aware of what could and could not be said, not arguing with him about any issue, not asking for anything, and generally treating him as somebody who needed his own space to do what he had to do to provide for the family.

My mother, on the other hand, had the responsibility of bringing us up, and we had to ask her for anything we needed. Her word was final. I know this sounds rather like a dictatorship, but it was not. There were clear-cut roles and responsibilities. Everybody knew and respected their boundaries and the family structure worked well. There was respect where respect was due and plenty of love to go round. We were never without love or material things. The system worked to give us rewarding lives.

My brothers and sister were all loving and caring towards each other. As the eldest, I had to set a good example to the rest. No pressure there! We were one close, loving and happy family. As the years went by, all these relationships changed, with each sibling pursuing his or her own path. Working together in the family business made these relationships difficult in later years, and they remain strained even today.

Our intentions, motivations and demands change when we get married and have children of our own. We sometimes expect the same life that we enjoyed before marriage. We like stability and find change difficult to manage. We stop planning, and become comfortable with the status quo. Why fix something that is not completely broken? Sure, we see the cracks opening up, but we turn a blind eye to them. It happens in every family, we say. The cracks will repair themselves. They never do; they only getter bigger and deeper, until it is too late to do anything about them. Sadly, even today we have two "groups" of siblings, neither speaking to the other.

And the longer you leave it to fix things, the worse it gets, perhaps to a point of indifference and nonchalance. How did we get this angry and intolerant towards each other? Why did we allow a wedge to be driven between us, one so deep that the mere effort needed to remove it seems impossible? I suspect we get so used to this new status quo that changing it seems a herculean task, too much of a bother. Who needs them? we ask. We have a good life; who needs the aggro? We have become complacent and lazy.

Somehow, we had forgotten the importance of *sewa* and *sangat*. Forgotten the roots that had nourished us so well for so long. Funny thing about fundamentals, basics or roots: we have to identify what they are for ourselves. They form the platform from which we attempt to excel in whatever we do, be it in sport, writing, careers, relationships, or diet.

Sewa takes us to our fundamentals. As with the basics in sport, they need to be visited and practised regularly, so that they become the memory and reference point for our wider training, or living. "Never neglect your basics" is a regular mantra of sports teachers. We may do well to apply this to our lives. I would suggest that *sewa* contributes to the platform that helps us choose how to live our lives.

The first few years of married life were great. We started building a family of our own. Life became a roller coaster. Lots of parties, networking, drinking and eating, never realising that most of my time and attention was on work. I had become a workaholic, and my family became secondary.

I did not realise that my wife had become a sort of slave to me, to feed me and to bear my children and look after them. There was no time to ask her about her dreams, inspirations and feelings. Life seemed to work best for me, so why look for anything that would rock the status quo? I was happy and exhilarated about being me, just thinking with my head, busy unconsciously building my ego and placing it on a pedestal.

Everything at home had to revolve around me. I was the master and the provider. Everything was OK; after all, she didn't complain. She looked and seemed to be happy. No need to dig deeper. That was the intention, because it suited me. I needed to provide, and nothing else mattered – or so I thought. Time would teach me a lesson about life and about what really mattered.

But right then I was riding high on success and priming myself for a major heart attack. I had become deaf and blind to all that was around me. Life is too short, I would think, so make the most of it while you can. Work, eat, drink, live and let live.

Don't get me wrong. I did not intentionally go out of my way to make life difficult for her. We had lots of fun together, made each other laugh and worked to provide the children with a decent education. They always had the best birthday presents, outings for picnics and fairs, and anything they asked for. But my intentions were all wrong. I realise that now with a lot of regret. I wanted to be the best husband and father, son and brother, but it had to be on my terms. I know I sound like a monster to you right now, but that is the way it was. As I said, my life revolved around actions taken with the wrong intentions.

We value being busy and find it difficult to find quiet time for reflection. We are constantly reminded that it is important to seek personal success – the exterior is more important than what is inside. We easily become disconnected from ourselves and make life complicated.

If we valued simplicity, our lives would become simple. We would recognise that there is an order to all things and that we are in harmony with ourselves and life. There is a divine order. It determines the rhythm of life. Look at nature. The plants and animals know this.

I had to make my life simpler by recognising there is an order to all existence. I had to stop using my cunning to outsmart the natural order of the divine. I had to recognise the *sangat* and, through *sewa*, seek spiritual guidance from those who have recognised and surrendered to the rhythm of life. *Sewa* helped me to reconnect with my own inner source of spiritual wisdom. I realised that there had always been a plan for me. I had just got side-tracked by my busy-ness.

As I relate these past experiences, I am reminded of the following poem by Lao Tzu.

> He who stands on tiptoe doesn't stand firm.
> He who rushes ahead doesn't go far.
> He who tries to shine dims his own light.
> He who defines himself can't know who he really is.
> He who has power over others can't empower himself.
> He who clings to his work will create nothing that endures.
> If you want to accord with the Tao,
> just do your job, then let go.

I had not been participating in life but had been busy building solid walls for my ego. I had not learnt to live life. Everything I had done up to that point was an act that had an accompanying mood. But a near-death experience and reflection about the certainty of death raised stark realities that I could not hide or shy away from.

Don Juan says the following to Castaneda (Journey to Xtlan: The Lessons Of Don Juan):

> Think of your death now. It is at arm's length. It may tap you [at] any moment, so really you have no time for crappy thoughts and moods. None of us have time for that. The only thing that counts is action, acting instead of talking.

I cannot argue with that.

As I recovered from my heart attack, I was glad she stuck around. I don't want to speculate why. I don't want to feel any worse than I do now. I had to reconnect to *sangat* and *sewa*. Initially this feeling was based on the notion that the heart attack was a result of having ignored these divine principles with which I had been brought up. It was also a partial response to the challenge "You have been given a second chance; don't repeat your old mistakes; get rid of the ego".

Vanquishing something that I had begun to develop the day I was born seemed a frustrating and impossible task. I became obsessed with executing the enemy within. I was really hard on myself and, as each effort resulted in failure, I ended up with more and more harsh self-criticism. I began to hate myself, to hate who I was, to feel guilty about my very person.

As I reconnected with *sangat* through *sewa*, and travelled the path, with Guru's grace, I realised that I had to cut myself some slack in order to open up to all possibilities.

> *Vichi duneeaa sev kamaaeeai. Taa dargahi baisan paaeeai.*
> ("In the midst of this world, do selfless service [*sewa*], and you will attain the experience of Divine Realm. Then, says Nanak, you will become free from all worries.") (*SGGS*)

You may know the story about the jar of life-stones, pebbles and sand. An old professor filled an empty jar with large stones. Everybody said the jar was full. No, said the professor, and brought out the pebbles and sand.

What can we learn from this? The important lesson is that, if we don't put the larger stones into the jar first, we will never be able to fit them all in later. Sadly, we give priority to the smaller things in life (the pebbles and sand). Our lives get filled up with less important things, leaving little or no time for the things in our lives that are most important to us. What are the large stones in your life? Wealth, family, friends, love, health …?

I am also reminded of the wise words of Lao Tzu, who said in the *Tao Te Ching*:

> Simplicity, patience, compassion. These three are your greatest treasures. Simple in actions and thoughts, you return to the source of being. Patient with both friends and enemies, you accord with the way things are. Compassionate towards yourself, you reconcile all beings in the world.

As the thinking, strategising person in me faded into the background, an inner light began to filter through the fog of years of conditioning. I didn't need to be obsessed to kill the ego but, rather, to learn to recognise and respond to it appropriately.

The ego has begun to become a friend now. Now I lust for the company of *sangat*, and to direct energy previously wasted on anger towards developing more compassion and understanding. I am attached to the journey of self-discovery, effortlessly learning and understanding more about the *sangat* through *sewa* around me.

The following extract from the Sikh *ardhas* pays homage to those who, despite being tortured to death, were true to themselves. They sacrificed their lives for freedom of expression so that everyone can live fulfilling lives as they wish, free from the shackles of authoritarian tyranny and the tyranny of conditioning.

> *Jinhaan singh-aan singhnnee-aan ne dharam haet sees ditae,*
> *band band kattaa-ae … tinhaan dee kamaa-ee da dhiaan*
> *dharkae, khaalsaa jee, bolo jee Waheguru .* ("Let us give our
> praise to the same, to all the masters, warriors, saints, and
> sages, to all those who sacrificed throughout the ages … they
> gave life to Sikh Dharma with the power of their death. Khalsa
> Ji Sahib, Bolo Ji, Siri Waheguru.")

We can learn from the sacrifices of others. Their *sewa* to humankind allows us the freedom of expression to live fulfilling lives that may be different but are of equal morality, integrity and honesty.

We may wonder how people can suffer such horrors. As with everything, life has a duality. The impossible becomes possible because of our heartfelt belief and deep commitment. This is how people cross the ocean on a raft. Risking death so that their children do not die in the war at home. It is how you stand in front of a tank to protest against torture and dare to be shot. It is how you shun fame and wealth and live with the poor and helpless, because one person's suffering is your suffering. *Sewa* and *sangat* combine to help you move past the ego.

Sewa provides me with direct experience of recognising the *sangat*. It is no longer an academic exercise, based on concepts, ideas and intellectual understanding. It is contentment based not on helplessness or hopelessness, but that comes from saying, "Thank you, for you have given me more than I need".

"I don't know what your destiny will be, but one thing I do know: the only ones among you who will be really happy are those who have sought and found how to serve," said the French-German theologian and philosopher Albert Schweitzer (1875–1965).

I had learnt that there were only two ways of living: one that is self-centred and one that is selfless. The challenge is to recognise which of these we are living, simply because we can rationalise any behaviour to make sense of our worlds. We call it survival of the fittest. You have to do what you have to do to get ahead. But ahead to where?

We all aspire to be something, somewhere. Living in the future. Unwittingly, building a strong cage around us. Life gets constricted. Our aspirations become distant. We blame others. It gets suffocating and life becomes tiring. Always trying to catch up. In fear. The realisation dawns that you have become self-centred.

At some point in life, we get weary and overwhelmed. The burden becomes unbearable. Anxiety, hardship and desperation set in. We feel let down by people we relied upon. We feel abandoned and alone. We feel incomplete.

But we pick ourselves up and endure. Things change, improve. We learn and move on. And then it happens again. We get weary and overwhelmed. The cycle repeats itself. As does the roller coaster of happiness and unhappiness. Of hope and desperation. Of completeness and incompleteness.

There is another way of living – the Guru's way that fulfils your every dream and beyond. To be liberated all the time. To live in the moment, not some projection into the future. Now, in your fullest self, the spirit. Serving the Guru by listening and practising the teachings. Serving the Guru through service to others. Serving by being honest in your dealings. Serving by loving all, regardless of their inclinations. Serving by trusting the Guru. Liberated. Fearless. Like the *naam*. Like the *shabad*. Spontaneous. Selfless.

Through *sewa* and *sangat*, I sought the sanctuary of my Guru. The enduring love of the Guru never leaves me for a moment amid all my trials and tribulations. I knew my Guru would make me whole again. There was no need to sell myself short. I knew somehow that he was not going to let me fail after taking me this far.

Remember all the battles you have already won and the fears you have overcome. However small, take the next step. You know where you are now. Get closer to where you want to be.

This *shabad* beautifully captures *sewa* and all that comes with it:

> *Jat sat tap pavit sareeraa har har mann vasaaye.* ("One who serves the Satguru obtains *jat* [restraint of the mind and the senses], *sat* [realises the truth] and *tap* [focus or one-pointedness of the mind]; his body is purified and the Lord's name comes to dwell in his mind.") (*SGGS*)

Guru ji, guides us, through sewa and sangat, to develop *spiritual traits* that embed within us the courage to follow the path set out by his teachings.

Chapter 3

Ardhas – A Prayer for Seeking Grace and Saying "Thank you"

Jeea Kee Birathhaa Hoe S Gur Pehi Ardhas Kar. Shhodd Siaanp
Sagal Man Than Arap Dhhar

"Regarding thy mind's woes, make supplication before thy
guru. Forsake thou all thy cleverness and dedicate unto him
thy mind and body." (*SGGS*)

The stark realisation that life can be over without a moment's notice
and that I wasn't powerful and invincible after all pushed me into
a place from where there was no escape. My reference points for
making sense of my well-being, the intentions and purposes in my
life, understanding how others lived and the wider world, all seemed
to be irrelevant and meaningless. All that was left was prayer.

We had emigrated from Kenya only two months before I had the
heart attack. I had a wife and young family to support in this strange
country. We wanted to make a fresh start and build a new life. But
now I could see my pre-set horizons flicker … blur … and fade
away. The next phase of my journey had been stopped before it had
begun. I had yet to see and understand.

It is April 1996, and we have just landed at Heathrow airport. As the
plane is about to come to a halt, passengers have already begun to
get out of their seats, so as to be the first off. Everybody is always in
a rush; we always have to be somewhere else than where we are.
We feel very restricted and suffocated when we have to sit still for a
while. When we are free from the constraints of the plane, we feel

the need to get away from it as soon as possible. Away from all the strangers with whom we started conversations.

As my family and I remain seated waiting for the mad rush for the exit, I notice a tall, well-dressed man with a tie and confident gait getting up from his seat, reaching for his luggage from the overhead compartment. I notice that he has a laptop and executive luggage. I think, *He's a high flyer*. For some reason, I am drawn to this total stranger, wondering what he does for a living. Later, as we come out of the terminal, I see the same gentleman introducing himself to a chauffeur holding a placard with his name on it. I am envious of him. Bertrand Russell wrote in *The Conquest of Happiness* about deriving pain from what others have, instead of pleasure from what we ourselves have.

And at that moment I prayed and wished I was him – a high flyer in a chauffeur-driven limousine. Little did I know that someone out there was reading my thoughts and that, within a couple of years, my life would be so changed that I would be flying in and out of European airports. I would see my own name on a placard and be transported in a chauffeur-driven car. For that to happen, I had to go on a journey that would begin two months later with a heart attack.

It is true that prayers come true, but before that happened I had to learn to face myself honestly, to learn to pray from a space deep within. To face yourself honestly takes a lifetime of effort. You have to see yourself in what you do and how you live, to learn about yourself. Bruce Lee talked about this. How it is easy to do things that impress people and reassure ourselves, but they are not what sustains a martial artist. To face yourself and not rely on high kicks or fast punches for self-worth. This is the journey of the martial artist. When you begin to face yourself honestly, your reference points of who you are and how you live change. All the external transient events around us become secondary to what is constant and sustains. The light inside us; call it and feel it as you will.

I had always known about "prayer". I had on countless occasions prayed for a new car, a fantastic holiday, (more) money, and so on; always asking for things, like a child at Christmas. I did pray when I had the heart attack and I remember it went something like this: "I don't know what I have done to deserve this. Why me? What I have ever done to You?"

Dutch Sheets, author of the international bestseller *Intercessory Prayer: How God Can Use Your Prayers to Move Heaven and Earth*, says: "Prayer is not a check [cheque] request asking for things from God. It is a deposit slip – a way of depositing God's character into our bankrupt souls." As I recovered from the heart attack in hospital, the "why me?" questions flowed freely as I wallowed in self-pity. Somebody was responsible for this – not me, no sir, but somebody else. The first on my list was God. I had been brought up in a Sikh household and had always followed the ritualistic visits to the temple at least once a week. I had prayed every day, even when I had been drunk and suffering a hangover. I was a nice person (I really believed that then).

So, what had gone wrong? Why this punishment from God? A fickle mind with an ego to match can be a dangerous thing. I finally solved this riddle, or so I thought. As a Sikh, I shouldn't have been drinking alcohol and trimming my beard (one of the main tenets of the Sikh religion is unshorn hair). That was it! This was the punishment. It sounds silly now, but I assure you that a near-death experience throws up lots of straws to cling to. This had to be rectified. I promised God – through prayer, of course – that I would stop these bad habits right away and that I would undergo the Sikh baptism, *amritsanchaar*.

The trouble was that, as I got better, the promises faded away, not helped by the doctor's advice that red wine was good for the heart. After a week in intensive care I was moved to the general ward, where there were three other patients who had suffered heart attacks. I was allowed visitors, as were the others.

Forgotten were the promises to God and the visit of the Sikh warrior spirits. My mind said, "You have to look good for the visitors" because, somewhere at the back of my mind, I felt like a hero who had cheated death. Friends and family would be coming to see me and I had to look smart. It sounds really fickle to me now and I am embarrassed to admit it, but that was the level of my consciousness – completely blurred in a thick fog of my ego. I asked for a pair of scissors to trim my beard.

But then a number of events occurred on the general ward that created cracks in my bloated ego. There was an elderly patient, waiting for an angiogram. He never had visitors, but one day he received a phone call from one of his sons to say that he would visit. The man looked elated, but the son never showed up. The man was visibly upset. The following evening, he passed away. At the end, he accepted what was. There was no choice. He had nurtured a family and set lives moving for them. This was their gift, the opportunity to learn about the need for *sangat*, and the importance of *sewa*. By the grace of God.

A second patient passed away during a coronary bypass operation. He had been very upbeat, full of plans for the future. His dreams melted away into the unknown darkness. The third person was a very pleasant gentleman who had suffered a second heart attack. Strangely, he told me his family did not even know he was in hospital. He would just take the bus home upon his release. What courage, I thought; he is treating his illness as if he had the flu. How do we become like that? So fearless? It reminded me of Oliver Sacks, and how he responded to being diagnosed with cancer:

> I cannot pretend I am without fear. But my predominant feeling is one of gratitude. I have loved and been loved; I have been given much and I have given something in return; I have read and traveled and thought and written. I have had an intercourse with the world, the special intercourse of writers and readers. Above all, I have been a sentient being, a thinking animal, on this beautiful planet, and that in itself has been an enormous privilege and adventure. (*New York Times*, 19 February 2015)

This series of events around me shook me to the core. I realised that I could have been any one of the men. I took for granted all the love and care surrounding me. I felt I deserved to be treated like royalty, treating my loved ones as subjects. The realisation that I had not loved back hit me like a ton of bricks. What was wrong with me? What had I become?

I was surrounded by the love of my wife and children, had every whim and wish attended to, and all I could think of was how to get back to being the same person I had been before. Was I that self-centred and conceited? I was harsh with myself. There is something we all need. Oliver Sacks again:

> To live on a day-to-day basis is insufficient for human beings; we need to transcend, transport, escape; we need meaning, understanding, and explanation; we need to see over-all patterns in our lives. We need hope, the sense of a future. And we need freedom (or, at least, the illusion of freedom) to get beyond ourselves, whether with telescopes and microscopes and our ever-burgeoning technology, or in states of mind that allow us to travel to other worlds, to rise above our immediate surroundings. We may seek, too, a relaxing of inhibitions that makes it easier to bond with each other, or transports that make our consciousness of time and mortality easier to bear. We seek a holiday from our inner and outer restrictions, a more intense sense of the here and now, the beauty and value of the world we live in. (From "Altered States: Self-experiments in Chemistry", *The New Yorker*, 27 August 2012)

There is a saying that you should become the change you want to see in the world – you find out who you are first, then your vision will be clear enough to see what needs to be done.

I had yet to learn that the prerequisite to *ardhas* was total surrender, an acceptance that you really are not in control. I still had to learn that to receive I needed to be open. To be open to what is being given and not to reframe it, filter it, reinterpret it – to really accept it as it is given, completely, without fear, with gratitude.

In short, I needed to grow, to be renewed by seeking and understanding within. I had sought the events that had come and gone outside. This did not make sense to me any more, because I had not looked within me at what is always there guiding my well-being. *Sangat* and *sewa* would prepare me, show me the way and sustain me. The journey would be as hazardous as any taken by an explorer. I wanted to be true to how *ardhas* should be done.

In the Sikh *ardhas* there is an invocation: *Sikha da maan niva math ochi mat pata da rakha app Waheguru*. The essence of this is "Let me seek answers with an open heart and mind, let me not expect what I believe I need; instead, help me trust in the value of what is offered".

I had to learn that the universe puts you in the company of those who will benefit you and be benefited by you; and that I could draw upon this abundant resource if my prejudices didn't function as a curtain that distorted everything. I had to learn to be silent in order to listen. And then allow the silence to lead me.

Through *sewa*, I gradually put my prejudices aside and began to find an immense synchronicity in all those with whom I came into contact. A harmony with others in the form of *sangat* that led me gently towards my own natural evolution and realisation that the universe is full of unconditional love and compassion. Constant companions, always nudging me to success and happiness. It only asks you to acknowledge and do the same.

The cause of human suffering is the illusion that we are what we associate with, do or think. We attach our mind and body to events, feelings and objects as if they are central to our existence. We know they are transient and do not necessarily control our lives, but still we put our faith in them, even when they lead us to inevitable disappointment. Our culture, religion, friends, society, family and education all contribute to our beliefs and perceptions.

If we lose our connection with this timeless and universal part of us – love – we live as victims of the changing winds of life; never realising that it is the love inside us and between us that has been constant, brought us here and kept suffering at bay. Keeping that connection tunes us, like a musical instrument, to have a clearer perception and to see beyond physical associations to what helps our deeper being and soul so that we can live by associating with the protective, compassionate, nurturing and constant divine light within. To keep on the straight and narrow.

This means to be have morals; to follow a path of honesty and integrity. Most often, we are led to this path after experiences from walking on a much broader path that is strewn with obstacles. Disappointments. Failures.

The power of *ardhas* keeps us, keeps me, steadfast on the straight and narrow path (*"khanni-ahu tikhee vaalahu nikee ayt maarag jaanaa"* – Anand Sahib). It had been destined to be so. I and you have earned it, by practising the wisdom of our Guru. A wisdom that has imbued my character with compassion, selflessness, service to others, justice, equity and fearlessness.

In every moment, I live my life with the understanding that I am in the embrace of the Guru. I am already blessed. My journey has culminated at this point because my Guru wished it to be so. I have faith that I am being looked after in every moment of my life. All I need to do is stay on the path shown by Guru Ji. The straight and narrow.

> Enter ye in by the narrow gate: for wide is the gate, and broad is the way, that leadeth to destruction, and many be they that enter in thereby: For narrow is the gate, and straitened is the way, that leadeth unto life, and few be they that find it. (*Matthew 7:13–14*)

And that is true prayer, *ardhas*, giving constant thanks to your Guru, safe in the knowledge that you need not ask for anything, because all that is needed will be provided without your asking. Why is it important that you are with God and God alone on the mountain top? It's important because it's the place in which you can listen to the voice of the One who calls you the beloved.

Henri Nouwen (1932–96), a Dutch Catholic priest, professor, writer and theologian, wrote:

> To pray is to listen to the One who calls you "my beloved daughter", "my beloved son", "my beloved child". To pray is to let that voice speak to the centre of your being, to your guts, and let that voice resound in your whole being.

This is how I try to lead my life. I recite the *ardhas* every day and accept the outcome. I don't demand anything and am content with what is provided. It is as simple as that. Sikhs call it *gurprasad* (seeking the Guru's grace) and *hukam* (accepting the outcome). Accepting whatever life gives me with deep gratitude, knowing that grace embraces me very moment of my life.

As a young boy, I used to watch countless movies about treasure hunters looking for either the fountain of youth or everlasting life. The movies were full of adventures: monsters, crossing angry oceans, mystical creatures and spirits guiding the hero, moments of desperation, moments of bliss, moments of success and failure. It required determination, cunning and single-mindedness (and a pretty girl in the mix). The movies ended with the destruction of the magic potion. A wasted journey.

We are all looking for the elixir of everlasting life. The elixir of immortality. The philosopher's stone. The mystical potion that grants the drinker everlasting life and everlasting youth. What is the secret of everlasting life?

Guru Ji gives us this elixir. We don't have to be alchemists trying to formulate the elixir with all our clever strategies, manipulations, struggles and cunning. There is only one monster to fight: our attachment to *Maya* (the pretty girl in the movie). Free yourself from these entrapments by recognising that you are already an eternal being. The spirit (*mool*). The elixir. Every act and thought springing from pure love.

Let us deconstruct words like ambition, success, achievement, vision, aspirations. What is the underlying driver for all these? On the surface, it might seem that they are means to an end. But what is that end? Is it fame, power, control, love, freedom? What do these mean? Happiness, contentment and security at the end of the journey?

Let us dig even further. We are not really in control of the paths we choose to walk on. There are others involved, too. Some who challenge us, pull us down, stop us. Others who give us a helping hand. Some who might even walk with us. Still others who give us wrong directions. We are never sure. Uncertain. Fearful. The outcome of our efforts depends on others. Not always getting our way. *It's not fair*, we often say. The path feels stressful and painful. Where is the justice in this?

What if we started at the end? Be happy, content and secure first. And then travel the journey of ambition, success, achievement, vision and aspirations. *That is the way you should do it,* Guru Ji says. Make Him your spirit, your being, your constant companion. Then the journey becomes the end. There is no difference between them. You become the experience. Never feeling let down or fearful. Let that be your *ardhas.*

We seek guidance when feeling let down, in despair, hurt, in failure, or in sickness. Always when we are at our lowest point. But these are times when we seek guidance to serious questions. Questions like "Who am I?" and "What is life?".

What drives us to seek guidance when at our lowest point? Isn't it a feeling of vulnerability, helplessness, fear, or isolation? When we do get the guidance, we recover but fall into the same trap again. This is also true for those who seek answers to the more serious questions. Why? Because, Guru Ji says, we live our lives as if asleep, or like zombies. Without inspiration and with limited interest. Always seeking a quick fix.

Guru Ji says that our quest for living should be full of positive actions. Of being brave and believing in the guidance of the Guru. A simple guide for developing a character of compassion, humility, selflessness and courage. Of living life fully awake, totally aware and constantly inspired. Avoiding the company of people who walk in their sleep, slandering others because of their beliefs. Be in the company of those (*gurmukh*) who live their lives fully awake. Not feeling vulnerable, helpless – in the company of the beloved (your spirit).

I have given up making demands of the universe. No entitlement, just humility and gratitude that come from being in the embrace of love. I have no expectations, and am open to what life brings to me daily. I enjoy life as it presents itself and am thankful for the surprises that the remembrance of His name gives me.

To me – and this is important – the use of words such as "Your name" (commonly used in many religions), "*naam*" (mostly used in Sikh and Hindu *dharma*) or "Will" or "God" translates simply as a limitless well of unconditional love, love without labels or expectations. Through this arise opportunities, experiences, and

49

realisations of contentment for oneself and compassion for others. You and I and everyone else we know and meet is capable of the same unconditional love. This is the path of *dharma*. This is *ardhas* in the truest form. Being thankful for this immense power.

There is a Sikh *shabad* that moves me whenever I pray:

> *Mai kia maago kichu thiru na rahai.* ("What should I ask for? Nothing remains permanent.") (*SGGS*)

I have a feeling that the practice of *dharma* must be a fundamental law of the universe, or the planet wouldn't have survived this long. People engage in constant tirades about the demerits of teachings of all religious texts because they believe that their suffering is a consequence of the actions of others. But if we remember that God is nothing but love, we would be practising *dharma*. This begins where all religious paths end. Yes, it is important to walk on a chosen religious path. But don't get stuck on that path. Keep practising the teachings.

Throughout our lives, we accumulate experiences. Our perceptions of ourselves are dependent on our experiences. And there are times, especially as we get older – more experienced – when we begin to walk with stooped shoulders. We get overburdened. Sometimes we reach breaking point.

We label these points as psychological in nature and seek interventions accordingly, to drill down into the psychological mind to seek out the source of our suffering or unhappiness. But Guru Ji offers us another way. No matter what burden you carry, it is never too late to come to the Guru. He won't judge you.

But there is one condition. It is to practise the teachings of the Guru. Just listening or going to the *gurdwara* is not quite enough. The word "praxis" comes from the Greek via medieval Latin – and means doing, or action, from *"prassein"*, to do or practice (Merriam-Webster). Meditating (*jap, simran*) is the praxis of the teachings of the Guru. It begins with total trust in the Guru. With prayer (*ardhas*). Drop the weight from your shoulders. Be light. Seek the grace of the Guru.

Take actions (*simran*) that begin with forgiving yourself and others, improve your communication (tone down your language), start listening, understand the other's point of view, smile at strangers, say thank you, stop judging, extend your hand to others, etc. All these are but attributes of love. This is how you serve Him. Practise these and experience *Waheguru* everywhere.

I had to let go of my pre-heart attack self in order to receive grace; to drop my preconceptions, my conditioning, for the realisation to dawn that I was already worthy. I know the meaning of *apna mool pechan*.

Electricity (energy) follows the path of least resistance. The shortest distance between two points is a straight line. These are proven scientific truths. All perceptions, thoughts, emotions and experiences are expressions of "*maya*". *Maya* is fluid. Don't try to straighten it by digging deeper into it (resistance). Choose the path of the Guru (*hukam* – acceptance that it cannot be better than this moment). The path of least resistance. Direct connection. This is the Guru's message. To be in constant remembrance.

Begin by no longer listening to the mind-body (*maan*, thoughts). Follow the *hukam* of the Guru. Take responsibility for your actions. Do not harbour evil intentions against others. Go beyond habits. Focus on the moment, break from the past (*atit*). Don't look back – no baggage (*sadh ko milan jayay, sath na lejay koi* – Kabir). Experiences do not happen in time and space. They happen in the "now", the "here". Living in the "here", the "moment", the "now" is living in the constant company of the Guru (*mool*, spirit, *hukam*). Straight line.

A year after my heart attack, I was given the gift of *amrit* (Sikh baptism) and, for the first time in my life, felt the presence of my Guru around me. I went back to university at the age of 41 and successfully completed an MSc degree and a PhD.

I do not prepare for everything and plan every detail. Instead I converse with life, have a love affair with my heart and never forget to give thanks. That is my *ardhas* for you, *Sarbat the Bhalla*.

I would like to share these two lines from two *shabads* on *ardhas* that are important to me.

> *Birthi kade na hovoi jan ki ardhas.* ("The prayer of the God's slave goes not in vain.") (*SGGS*)

> *Jojo kahai thakur pahi sevak tat kal hoi avai.* ("Whatever the servant asks his Master, forthwith comes to pass.") (*SGGS*)

But there are conditions.

> *Mai nahi kichh hao nahi kichh ahe na mora.* ("I am nothing and nothing is mine.") (*SGGS*)

I had to let go of my imagined powers and identity. And that meant no longer trying to be clever in order to fool the universe. Benjamin Franklin, one of the Founding Fathers of the United States, provided a wonderful perspective when he said, "Work as if you were to live a hundred years, pray as if you were to die tomorrow".

The Guru's message is simple. Have the courage to stand out from the crowd. It is OK to be different. Be faithful to your Guru by being merciful, courageous, fearless. Love life as you would a wonderful play. Live in his *neeyam* (the Guru's law). When you blend in, you create your own messenger of death (*yam* – your next reincarnation body). Those who stay within the *neeyam* never create *yam*. They are blessed and liberated. Guru ji reminds us of the genie within us. Always ready to grant unlimited wishes. Just like in the fable, we must clean the lamp to release the genie. All we need to do is seek his grace through *ardhas*.

That is my *ardhas*. And it is only the Guru that can make it happen. Every Sikh, who has been to a wedding, knows these lines by heart.

> *Kita lorhiai kamu su Hari pai akhiai. Karaj dei sawari satgur sachu sakhai.* ("Whatever work thou desirest to do, tell that to the Lord. He shall accomplish thy affair. The True Guru bears true testimony of it.")

And that is the power of *ardhas*.

Chapter 4

Jap and *simran*

Saasath Sinmrith Baedh Beechaarae Mehaa Purakhan Eio
Kehiaa. Bin Har Bhajan Naahee Nisathaaraa Sook N Kinehoon
Lehiaa

"The great men after the study of the Shastras, Simiritis and
Vedas, have said the following: 'Without God's meditation
there is no emancipation, nor has any one attained peace'."
(SGGS)

It's July 2007 and it has been eleven years since the heart attack.
A lot has happened since. I had gone back to university for my
postgraduate studies. Later, I worked in academia as a researcher
and on several European research projects. Now as the regional
director for East Africa of an NGO based in the Netherlands, fate
had brought me back to Kenya, my country of birth. I was managing
a poverty reduction project in the Highlands, and on this particular
day was accompanying a Dutch documentary crew, filming the
project on behalf of the project's sponsors.

As we reached the project area, we were welcomed by a group of
20 school children. They were dressed in tattered school uniforms,
and some of the children did not even have shoes. As the filming
began, they started singing in unison, gently swaying with the music.
They sang their hearts out, in a local dialect, with passion and hope
burning brightly in their eyes.

I was teary-eyed by the end of the song. The Dutch crew asked for a
translation. I had understood what they had sung:

> It was a dark and moonless light and we had gone to bed with
> little in our stomachs. In the middle of the night we heard a

loud knock on the door. We were frightened, but plucked up the courage to open it. As the door opened, we saw a bright light and in that light stood *dactari* ["doctor", a reference to me]. We could see hope and he helped us to get better. He taught us to be confident and believe in ourselves and love the land we are blessed with. He showed us the way. We pray for his long life.

The project had been going for about 18 months, but until this moment I had never realised its impact. These children had stripped me bare to the core, to my soul. I embraced them all and said, "No, don't say thank you, it's all your hard work, and your belief in yourself. Thank you all for giving me a chance, thank you for making me find myself."

But there was another reason I cried. My father, who I called "papaji", had told us about his own childhood and poverty. He was born around 1932 in a village in the Punjab, not unlike the village these children were singing in. He had come to Kenya as a young boy and had practically no skills to speak of. He came from a background of abject poverty.

In the hot summers, he used to recall, he and his brother would tie leaves to their feet when they crossed a dry sandy riverbed on the way to school because they could not afford a pair of shoes.

I must have seen him in the eyes of these young people and recognised, deep down, the hope and determination he must have had when he left his village in the Punjab as a young boy, following in the footsteps of my grandfather, who had made the same journey into the unknown a few years earlier.

Those first steps that my grandfather took so boldly out of his village to seek and secure a better future for his family laid the foundations upon which future generations built their lives. He was a gentle person – truthful, straightforward and a trusted member of the community. I am told that I am like him in many ways, but I think his shoes are too big for me to fill. I continue to make my best efforts through how I live to show that I value what he passed down to me.

Perhaps those very first steps that my grandfather took out of his village were no different to those I took to bring my family to the UK. Perhaps you are somehow always in the right place. Those first steps were, in a way, simple yet complete. He taught me a lot about what is worth striving for in life. "Seek not to follow in the footsteps of men of old; seek what they sought", wrote Matsuo Bashō (1644–94), a Japanese poet of the Edo period

My father had come to Kenya as a penniless young man. He learnt his trade as a motor mechanic, working in difficult conditions. The tree under which he began his career still exists today. It serves as a constant reminder of his humble beginnings. His loved this line in the Sikh *ardhas*: *Sikha da maan niva math ochi mat pata da rakha app Waheguru.* ("The Sikh's humble heart and noble thinking are sustained by you, my Lord.")

This is the same man who eventually built a successful business, owning his own house and two well-equipped motor repair workshops. He is the same man who sent me to a private university in the USA, the first person to do so from my town. He passed away in October 2015.

He was a wonderful father and provided well for his five children. He had a sixth child, a daughter who was adopted by my uncle and aunt because they could not have children of their own. That is the kind of man he was.

Funnily enough, this adopted child was born with a lot of good *karma*. A few years after her adoption, two children were born to my uncle. Later on in life when she got married, her good *karma* continued to bless her new family and she scaled the skies.

If she had not been "given away," perhaps we would have benefited from her *karma*. The point is that we are all connected, and these connections have a huge bearing on our physical, mental and spiritual states. The Punjabis have a saying that roughly translates into thanking and appreciating every connection you make and have (in your family, friends, associates, business and so on) because you never know whose *karma* is looking after you.

My father had a strong work ethic. He believed that the company accounts were the mirror of the business that reflected its performance. Every job that was carried out had to have a paper trail. And this man had no formal education!

He never missed a day's work in his life, no matter what challenges he faced, including ill health. He would repeatedly tell us that a working man should always report to his place of work on time, every working day, without fail – regardless of whether or not there was work.

He always drummed into us the logic that the right job should be given to the right person. If your business did not have the right personnel to do the job, either hire the right person or train one. He believed in treating his employees with dignity and respect. Employees were always asking for assistance and he always listened, ready to help them where he could. This was the purpose of his work, *sewa* – to make life better for those he loved, *sangat*.

Pause and reflect on these beautiful words penned by Kahlil Gibran:

> Work is love made visible.
>
> And if you cannot work with love but only with distaste, it is better that you should leave your work and sit at the gate of the temple and take alms of those who work with joy.
>
> For if you bake bread with indifference, you bake a bitter bread that feeds but half man's hunger.
>
> And if you grudge the crushing of the grapes, your grudge distils a poison in the wine.
>
> And if you sing though as angels, and love not the singing, you muffle man's ears to the voices of the day and the voices of the night.

These are words my father lived by. He was a far-sighted person and an excellent negotiator. He had to be, in order to enter into contracts with international construction companies building huge infrastructure projects such as roads, bridges, hydroelectric power stations and water treatment plants.

He loved to entertain, and there were always parties at our house attended by business partners, politicians, friends and family. He loved his food and made sure that his guests had the best. When he ate, he would patiently and lovingly fill his plate and place the plate with some deliberation in front of him before he began eating.

He would always remind us to treat the food in front of us with a lot of respect because "after all, this is what we are working for". His humble beginnings were never forgotten or lost in the wealth he had created. He always remembered his past, never brushing past the lessons of his journey from the village in Punjab and the abject poverty he had experienced.

My father had great expectations about us working together in the family business. This included my two younger brothers. He was an astute businessman who had, out of sheer hard work and tenacity, built a prosperous automotive repair business and a truck hire company that provided logistical support for international construction companies.

For us, it eventually proved to be a huge disappointment. This was compounded by the fact that we all lived together as an extended family. At one point, there were some 20 family members living under one roof. There was one common kitchen that catered for the tastes of all members of the family.

Eventually, as the families got bigger and demands greater, frictions began to build up. These finally reached a point where the business began to be affected, as did our personal relationships.

Perhaps building a degree of independence could have saved our relationships. Would this have made it possible to reach a compromise? The short answer is yes. We brought up our own children by instilling in them a spirit of individuality. To make their own mistakes and learn from them. To be better communicators, to express their feelings and emotions openly. With freedom of choice, but with us always there in the background to provide support if asked. Keeping an eye, but not interfering or forcing them to conform to a way of thinking, a lifestyle. To be able to make informed choices.

But what was different now, listening to these schoolchildren sing songs of praise? Why did I feel such humility and bliss? I had worked in the country for 30 years before emigrating to the UK and had run a successful business. I had never felt like this before. Nobody had shown such love and praise before.

The answer was simple. After the heart attack, *sangat*, *sewa* and *ardhas* had changed my inner being. Now I worked from a different place, deep within. The universe had prepared me for this moment and I had finally come home. I knew then and there that there was no separation between me and these children.

I remembered the gifts my father and all those I was fortunate to come across had given me. I also remembered the young doctor who had told my wife that there wasn't much hope of me surviving or having a full life. Yet here I was, more than ten years later, giving hope to others! I remembered the nurse who asked me to have the life-saving injection and the team of doctors who helped me along. I remembered my professors and supervisors who pushed a middle-aged man through university, gently nudging me forward, always encouraging, always giving hope.

I remember my mother, who gave us everything we needed and nourished me when I was a sick. I remember her for standing up and saying, "It's going to be OK," no matter what happened. I remember my teachers in primary school, who taught me values that serve me well every day. I think about my father, who gave me the gift of music. I remember my brothers and sisters, who gave so much love, but also remember with sadness the love lost. I remember my first love and the gift of love she unknowingly gave me. I remember all those who every day come into my life and show me that I am not alone. *We are here for you*, as I am for them.

I remember also those who annoyed me, pulled me back, stood in my way, insulted me and judged me. I love them for what they did because, without them, I would not have tried harder to become better and move forward.

The truth is that we are what we are because of the souls and experiences we have. We need to remember them, and thank them for their efforts and sacrifices. The universe has a plan for everyone, if only we can pause for a moment and see it.

In the Bhagavad-gita, one finds a record of Lord Krishna's words, spoken five thousand years ago in India. These form the essence of the Vedas, the knowledge of which propel the practitioner towards self-realisation. I would like to share one of these here. The Bhagavad Gita says "it's better to live your own destiny imperfectly than to live an imitation of somebody else's life with perfection". Yes, our forbearers set us on the path to greener pastures but isn't is exciting and wiser to follow one's own path, though imperfect, than the path of someone else, even though well-performed. I need not copy my father but rather use his wisdom to find my own special path.

"When you adopt the standards and the values of someone else," Eleanor Roosevelt wrote in her spectacular meditation on happiness and conformity, "you surrender your own integrity [and] become, to the extent of your surrender, less of a human being." Following even the highest standards is not enough. We need to be the light for the principles and values we are trying to live by.

This is *simran* on one level – an outer journey, always remembering and reminding oneself of where one came from. It's as simple as that, and not so difficult to do if you can put your prejudices aside and see them as *sangat*. If we cannot acknowledge and honour the people who come into our lives, how can we really discover our inner light? If we do not honour our parents, for example, how can we strive for loftier aspirations?

On another level, *jap* and *simran* – meditation or mindfulness – can also take us on an inner journey to seek the inner self. This is perhaps a more challenging matter.

Jap is about quietening the mind from the constant chatter going on within. It is estimated that a person has a thought every 1.9 seconds! *Jap* brings stillness of the mind. It provides a clarity of mind. Clarity is stability; the mind is silent.

Any thought that one keeps in mind in a state of silence is properly a command, since there are no other thoughts to compete with it (according to Don Juan).

Prior to the heart attack, through conditioning, I had become trained to rely on process thinking, trying to figure things out, treating life as a strategy. I had put too much technique and instruction into life.

However, the heart attack made me realise that I should accept life as whatever is it needs to be at that very moment – not being needy, planning and executing every moment all the time. This reflects a lack of faith in what is to come. We cannot live with this fear or worry. Use the following *shabad* as a guide: *Tu kahe dohle praania, tum rakhega sirjanhar.* ("Why do you let your spirit drop? The same love that brought you to here continues to take care of you.")

We are dealing with that immensity out there. To turn that magnificence into reasonableness doesn't do anything for you. Here, surrounding us, is eternity itself. To engage in reducing it to a manageable nonsense is petty and outright disastrous. Whenever the internal dialogue stops, the world collapses and extraordinary facets of ourselves surface, as though they had been kept under heavy guard by our words. You are like you are because you tell yourself that you are that way. You are too heavy and self-important. Let go! (Don Juan again.)

Doors open for us when we accept life as it presents itself. This is the outcome of *simran*. Then we have the space in our hearts and minds to feel gratitude for our lives. The gates open and release our guides for living: contentment, compassion and love.

In the *ardhas* there is another supplication: *Sikkhaan noon Sikkhee daan, kaes daan, rahit daan, bibbaek daan, visaah daan, bharosaa daan, daanaan sir daan, naam daan, Sree Amritsar jee dae ishnaan, chaunkee-aan, jhanddae, bungae, jugo jug attall dharam ka jaikaar, bolo jee Waheguru.* The gist of this invocation is a plea to God to grace the Sikh with the strength and wisdom to confer on the Sikh code of conduct divine wisdom, affirmation of the faith, unflinching belief and, above all, the treasure of spiritual identity including meditating *(simran)* upon the *naam* (the virtues of the Creator reflected in the various names assigned to Him – God, Waheguru, Ram, Allah, etc.) in the midst of life's responsibilities.

Intentions drive our actions in everyday life. The Guru's message is that spiritual intention (your Guru) should be driven by an unquestioned motivation to expand yourself beyond your everyday personal life (family, work, ambition).

Clarifying and focusing on your own true reason for "being" is one of the simplest yet most profound ways to cut through a lot of fragmented truths. Do this through *naam, jap, simran* and *ardhas*. Be in the company of the *sangat*. In this way, you will still your mind by allowing your focused spiritual intention (your Guru) to constantly guide all your actions.

Your focused spiritual intent, when made conscious, gives you a way to emulate your greater self, right here, moment by moment. Practising the qualities of your higher self with clarity (compassion, selfless service, forgiveness) moulds you into your Guru. It begins with a specific activity but later becomes a way of life.

We all have different enduring dispositions – the way we think, feel, act, perceive. It's called personality. But it is the type of personality we develop that is of great significance to the kind of Sikh (or Christian, Buddhist, Hindu, Muslim, human) we become. That is Guru Ji's message.

Any kind of person can be equally religious. We all think that what we believe and the way we do things is the best way; if not, we wouldn't believe those things or do things that way.

Guru Ji says it's OK to be different, to think differently, and to do things differently. But do all these things from your original self-knowing (spirit, *mool*). A place of compassion, forgiveness, oneness. That is the "personality" of your Guru. No judgement about your past actions. No punishment. Just surrender. Add these traits to your personality.

Mark Twain said that the two most important days of your life are when you were born and when you know why. We spend most of our time in between. Guru Ji reminds us of the "why". The time in between has been spent mostly being ungrateful (*kuchajee*).

Most of the time, personality rather than character forms our identity. Instead of defining ourselves through the cultivation of virtue, we define and express ourselves through material possessions, through conquest of the other (partner, children, colleagues). We give it the label "getting ahead". We don't develop moral values. We work on self-improvement. Self-sacrifice changes to self-realisation.

Guru Ji, through the practice of *simran*, builds our character instead.

The character of the Guru. Of our spirit. A character of compassion, love, forgiveness, sharing, non-judgement. Selfless. Such a character is grateful in every moment, no matter the outcome. The Greek word *kharakter* means "engraved mark" or "symbol or imprint on the soul". Discover why you were born.

We can agree that self-centredness and self-absorption are unappealing personality traits in a friend, colleague or partner. Guru Ji asks us to look at ourselves with the same critical eye.

Both self-centred and self-absorbed people are more concerned with their image and materialistic things. They don't bother to take the time to understand another person's point of view or feelings. Do we maintain a sense of compassion and understanding towards others? Do we complain or whine all the time, no matter what?

Understand that these traits are the cause of your suffering, Guru Ji says. Loosen their grip. Free yourself by realising that everything you see (*maya*) has been provided for us to use and to be fluid. Not to get stuck and become bitter. There is a plan for you (*hukam*). Stop being needy. Stop contracting yourself, limiting yourself. You are limitless.

Our own experience of – and not thinking about – any object, place, food or relationship imprints an impression within us. This implies intention and its execution. It means getting actively involved. Being present in the event providing the experience. To become the *simran*.

We need thoughts to act upon. Thoughts on their own have no power. The mind selects the ones it wants to act upon. We have the power to bring into existence our own reality by acting on the thoughts we choose. We can choose to have either a pragmatic mind or a psychological mind. It is our choice.

The pragmatic mind is our spirit's servant to do as commanded. The psychological mind, on the other hand, seeks to be the master (ego), always doing its own bidding. Never in one place (*trishna*, greed), always seeking acknowledgement (*ahankar*, pride). The pragmatic mind is grounded (*gurmukh*). Choose this path (intention) and walk on it (execute) with Guru Ji as your guide. Become present in your life. Become the experience. Be, and things become. That is the power of *simran*.

Through the practice of *simran*, I have begun slowly to develop an attitude that says, "If everything accumulates right here, if it does not go beyond this day or this moment, it is OK and good enough as it is". I am not waiting to arrive at a projected state.

And there is freedom in this - in trying to find out who you really are. When you have this urge, believe me, you find that the whole universe is helping you. *Gura ek dhe bhujai, sabna jia ka ek data so mai visaar na jhaie.* ("The Guru guides you to the realisation that there is only one God and he is omnipresent in all that exists in the universe. You are life itself! You are never alone.")

The following *shabad* soothes me and comforts me at all times, letting me know I am never alone:

> *Tati Vao na lagai parbrahm sarnai, Chaugird hamare ram kar dukhu lagai na bhai. Satguru pura bhetia jini banat banai. Ram nam aukhadh dia eka liv lai (rahao). Rakh lie tini rakhanhari sabh biadhi mitai. Kaho Nanak kirpa bhai Prabh bhae sahai.*

> ("Not even the hot wind touches him who is under the protection of the Supreme Lord. On my four sides is the Lord's circle, so pain afflicts me, not my brother. I have met the Perfect Guru, who has made everything. He has given me the medicine of the Lord's name and I have enshrined love for the One Lord. That preserver has preserved me and cured all my maladies. Says Nanak, 'the Lord has extended His mercy to me and has become my succourer'.")

Importantly, I have realised that you can't learn who you really are. You can only immerse in it. It is not learning by synchronicity. The simplicity of seeing who you really are is allowing it to be seen, to be experienced rather than through an intellectual exercise, or thinking, or figuring it out.

Through the practice of *jap* and *simran*, relax yourself, create the space within, for what you are seeking is in your heart, in your own being.

I discovered that spirituality is but the stripping away of all layers of conditioning. And that *simran* is a key tool for seeking my true self – pure love. *Simran* is like a ladder leading to the infinite, and the essence of worship.

When I am not, then there is One; when I intrude, then two. "When the curtain of 'I' and 'thou' is drawn aside, then do I become as I was [in the beginning]" observed Dadu, a Hindu-Muslim saint who inspired the formation of a sect called Dadu Panth.

Sangat, sewa, jap and *simran* washed my mind and stopped it from wandering. This created a wonderful glimpse of *anand* or bliss within me as I began to discover and realise the infinite soul, *mool*, within me. The practice of *jap* and *simran* then becomes the act of the infinite meditating on Himself, as expressed in this *shabad*:

> *Sargun nirgun nirankar sun samadhi api. Apan kia Nanaka appe hi phir jap.* ("The Formless Lord is Himself related and absolute. He himself is in a primordial trance. Nanak, through His own creation, He, again, meditates on Himself.") (*SGGS*)

We often hear the expression "We complement each other" and "You make me complete" when in love. It implies expectations. It is conditional. Based on circumstances. Looking for acceptance. Waiting to arrive at a projected state.

But moods, emotions, events and circumstances keep changing. Eventually, love runs its course. How do we navigate this maze? Where love is effortless. Unconditional. Guru Ji shows us how.

Begin by getting to know yourself. Be grateful to all the experiences and people you have met (good and bad). Without them you wouldn't have learnt anything. Acknowledge that there was a purpose to this. This is the first step to returning to your original self-knowing. Next, lift yourself by practising the teachings of the Guru (*naam, shabad*). Life will become a blessing in every moment. The rest falls into place without waiting to arrive at a projected state.

Jap and *simran* are the soul's voyage to discovery of its true *mool* and everlasting peace and commencement.

Chapter 5

Anand

Kabeer Man Niramal Bhaeiaa Jaisaa Gangaa Neer. Paashhai
Laago Har Firai Kehath Kabeer Kabeer

"Kabir, my mind has become immaculate like the water
of the Ganges. The Lord follows me saying, 'Kabir, O my
Kabir'". (*SGGS*)

Since the heart attack, I have been to hospital a number of times
for regular check-ups. But three of these visits in the last four years
have been particularly special because they were for very different
reasons. Gursharan and I became grandparents to three lovely souls.
We fell in love with them as soon as they were born. These blissful
moments themselves felt like gifts.

We felt gratitude, contentment and a lifting towards *anand*, or bliss.
I am not sure what else to say about this feeling or state. At this point
I find it helpful to think about Sean Meshorer, writing about his book
What is Bliss?

> *What is bliss?* It's a hard question. That isn't because bliss is
> vague, inchoate, or unreal, but rather because it surpasses
> the capacity of language. Bliss is so vast, boundless, and
> immeasurable that it encompasses every possible word or
> definition ever invented – and then some. This is, of course,
> why we continue to stress that bliss must be personally
> experienced, not just discussed. Like so many aspects of life,
> bliss is not readily apparent to our senses. Because bliss is
> not an object or a thing, our faculties of sight, hearing, touch,

taste, and smell are not designed to detect it. (From http://
seanmeshorer.com/what-is-bliss/)

In the past, I had come across a few souls who reminded me of
a more rewarding state of living, or *anand*. One such person was
Santa Singh, my wife's grandfather. He was a tall figure and one
of the purest souls I have met. He was a person of few words, but
had an aura, a presence, about him that projected simplicity and
honesty. He had come to Kenya as an eight-year-old in the company
of a few people from his village. He had worked very hard from that
young age – pure physical labour in the mines of Kakamega and on
the untamed land of Kibos, where he finally settled.

His wife, Gurnam, was a tough woman who had mettle and grit.
She was a woman who understood and accepted her responsibility
for her family. She supported her husband every step of the way, no
matter how tough, making sure it counted towards a better tomorrow.
She was the anchor of the family, with a very entrepreneurial spirit.

I see a lot of these qualities in my wife: patience, resilience,
calmness, generosity, endless love and compassion. She goes
without so that she can give to others. Each and every one of us
carries within habits and qualities of our forebears. She lives a life of
bliss, not fazed about what may come next.

I do not mean that she lives in the realm of God. That state is, of
course, deeper and detached from external events. I do not have
words for that. I do mean that her happiness is exceptional amongst
people, as I have seen. Little disturbs her balance and the natural
love she lives through and evokes in others.

After my attack, as I experienced the power of *sangat, sewa, ardhas*
and *sewa* I began to learn to live without trying to understand
everything. Learning not to be a slave to my thoughts but instead
recognising possibilities beyond those conjured up by the
conditioned mind. I began to be thankful for being able to open
my eyes every morning and experience life and whatever it brought
with it.

I began to constantly feel living in an embrace of love and to be
pleasantly surprised that I no longer worried about what would

come next. I now trust I will be led to what life wants of me and am no longer distracted by thoughts of what was or could be.

I surrender to them and then my relationship with the people and events in my life has changed from expectation to gratitude.

Gradually, as I delve deeper into my inner self, I begin to realise that I am not looking around in life for acceptance; there is no competition any more, no race to get somewhere, no desperate need to be something. I accept that life is whatever it needs to be.

Over the years following the heart attack, acknowledging the power and love of *sangat* all around me, carrying out *sewa* without any expectations, being thankful for each moment through *ardhas* and the constant practice of *simran* has provided me with experiences in life that gently nudged me along a path of original self-knowing. This beautiful and moving *shabad* comes to mind:

> *Sabh mah joti joti hai soiu. Tis dai channani sabh mahi chanan hoi. Gur sakhi joti pargat hoi.* ("Amongst all there is light and that light [art Thou]. By His light, the light shines within all souls. By the Guru's teaching the divine light becomes manifest.") (*SGGS*)

With the Guru's grace, as the path gets clearer and all fears and doubts fall away, I have begun to see life as a blessing in every moment. There is a natural trust and recognition that whatever is needed arises naturally, spontaneously, to meet whatever the needs of the moment are. The Guru, through his grace, is showing me glimpses of *anand*.

In my life before the heart attack, I realised I was a nobody, and now the Guru had lifted me to his bosom. I always get teary-eyed – even today, 20 years after surviving the attack – whenever I hear the following *shabad:*

> *Ham rulte phirte koi bat na puchhta. Gur Satgur sang keera ham thape.* ("I was rolling about in dust and no one cared for me. Through the association of the great True Guru I, a worm, am installed on [in] an exalted position.") (SGGS)

RECOGNISE YOUR LIGHT WITHIN - **APNA MOOL PECHAN**

In the past, so many things in life had engaged me to take different paths leading nowhere in particular. I was always trying to figure out this or that before I found the path to self-discovery.

I see a lot of these qualities of innocence in my grandchildren. The older has started nursery school and has begun to develop his own personality. We can all see the differences in his behaviour as he develops biases, opinions and concepts about his interpretation of life. And I can now see how these will eventually lead to more conditioning and mask the essence of him. It is my hope that my recent experiences and understanding will provide guidance as the grandchildren grow up, gently keeping them on the path to self-discovery.

Expectations should not have boundaries. I remember my schoolteachers, who always expected more from us than our abilities allowed. They did not know how much more we could know and understand, but we often surprised them by understanding ideas and demonstrating skills beyond their expert judgements about us.

Remember the saying that you should become the change you want to see in the world. But first you have to recognise your true self – the *joot saroop*, the eternal light – and then have the clarity of vision to see what needs to be done. Recognising your true nature and remaining anchored in it is *anand*; a state that provides you with an unchanging space within which everything happens – events, emotions, moods, work, family. All these are experienced by you as life, with no need to live the projections of other beings.

Anand is a state that goes beyond concepts. This is the awakened state bringing about the realisation that you are the infinite self and the life you are experiencing is a play of that infinite self.

In his Commentary on Chapter 2 of *The Secret of the Golden Flower: A Chinese Book of Life* (Richard Wilhelm translation), Carl Gustav Jung says:

> From the most ancient times till today, this is not empty talk, but the sequence of the Great Way in the true method of producing an eternally living and immortal spirit and holy man ... When the conscious spirit has been transformed into

the primal spirit, then only one can say that it has attained an infinite capacity for transformations and, departing from the cycle of births, has been brought to the six fold present, golden genius.

Anand is a state of complete contentment and peace. There are no demands on life any more; only acceptance of life and what it brings to you in spontaneity.

> Happiness as a path is all a matter of compliance; the way to bring about happiness is to be able to act in accord with the time. When one acts in accord with the time, the yang energy expands, so that all demons flee. The life-giving potential continues increasing, and the earth is always covered with yellow sprouts, the world blooms with Golden Flowers. Wherever one may walk, everywhere is the Tao. No happiness is more delightful than this. (Liu I-ming, *The Taoist I Ching*, Hexagram 16, Joy)

For me, the heart attack was a trigger to find inner peace. And to do that I would have to drop years of conditioning. I realised, after going through long periods of frustration, that knowing something and experiencing it were two completely different things.

More knowing inflated the ego; rationalisation provided comfort to the ego; for example, advertising to the rest of the world that "I did four hours of *sewa* and three hours of *simran* yesterday" took me further away from dropping my conditioning. The ego can show itself in so many ways. Arrogance, complacency, indifference, exaggeration, embellishment. Even humility can be arrogance. Intention from the heart is everything.

Though the Guru's grace I realised that I didn't need *more* knowledge, but perhaps the *right* knowledge. And I certainly did not need more experiences to have a realisation. All that was required was an earnestness for freedom, to drop at the feet of the Guru, and an *ardhas* that said, "Thank you for making me realise that there is more to me than my ego. I am ready to be guided from the innermost place. I surrender myself to your supreme authority."

Then I knew my heart was ready to remove the ignorance of decades of conditioning and move towards a realisation that everything that I needed was already within me. All I had to do was say "yes" to my Guru and allow him to speak directly to my heart.

"The body of pure yang was happy in the sun, the yin demons dared not use their might" appears in *Journey to the West*, a 16th-century Chinese novel attributed to Wu Cheng'en.

The mind, which was once always argumentative, opinionated, speculative and always personal, had to be quietened. This could only be done with the grace of the Guru, the absolute pure self. From the Guru came direct knowledge, *naam*.

The mind is always jumping for your attention to keep the amusement going. The most powerful thing for me was to be able take my attention away from the ego though *jap*, *simran*, *sewa* and *sangat*. It was a gradual process but, with Guru's grace, the mind began to quieten down to a point where thoughts faded away into the background. I could now choose the thoughts that required my immediate attention and ignore the rest. There was no need to have a technique and instruction to life. I was fine as I was.

This discovery and realisation unburdened me. I did not need to worry about anything because I trusted that every need would be taken care of. This is aptly expressed in this *shabad*: *"sail pathar may janth upae, agay rizek dhar rakhia"*. ("What is needed has already been provided, even before you were born.") If something was meant to happen it would. I did not have to control anything.

In the past, I had been contradicting my natural being. To see this is not an intellectual exercise; you just have to immerse yourself in it. It is not something you can force yourself to do. It comes from a complete surrender and total trust in your Guru.

The simplicity of seeing was allowing it to be seen, rather than through thinking or figuring it out. What I was seeking was always in the heart of my own being.

The truth is simple, but the seeker of truth is complex. It is only the ego that can be developed; your true identity cannot be developed

– it is already perfect, always has been, and always will be. You should honour the neutrality and the silence within you.

All you need to do is pause, take stock of your life and decide for yourself if your life has meaning to it. Do you want to chase success to strengthen the ego? If the answer is yes, then that is arrogance and can only lead to more suffering.

Or do you want to experience the state of *anand?* If the answer is yes, then go on a journey that takes you away from your conditioning and your mind towards a place deep within you where you find your *mool,* that is fearless, creativity itself, beyond knowledge, beyond judging, beyond physical death and pure intelligence. Blow away your ignorance and let go of all you have known. Success will follow without losing yourself.

Place your trust in the hands of the Guru, and be prepared to live a life beyond concepts, beyond processes. We are too used to taking actions. To be doing something. To be somewhere. Instead, observe a life without attachment, and develop the maturity to see events from both the physical and spiritual sides. You will discover contentment that comes from an underlying wisdom that guides your actions.

As you realise more about your inner self, you discover a natural trust and fearlessness. Countless doors, or possibilities, begin to open for you. Life becomes effortless. You don't hold onto any concepts and you become accepting of life as whatever it needs to be! You are no longer swimming upriver against the current. You go where the river of life takes you.

In the *anand* state, you don't hold on to any concepts but normal functioning continues. You function through labels, but that identity is temporary, for that moment only.

You no longer identify with the labels that restrict your being. You just play the role and move on to the next role, according to what life requires of you. You can be a parent in one moment, a businessperson in the next and a tennis player in the moment after that. You do your best in all these roles. But you are not stuck in the role. You know deep down that you are just the spirit, unaffected by any role-playing. You are always anchored in your *mool* and in a state of *anand*.

There is a natural trust and recognition that what is needed arises spontaneously to meet whatever are the needs of the moment. You are not dependent on the mind to do your bidding. The mind becomes a tool for you to do everyday things. It no longer sets the agenda of your life.

Now you use your mind for practical things. There is no psychological confusion about the thoughts that run amok in your head. You don't carry out any forensics on your thinking but just move on, trusting the light within you to guide you to whatever outcome life sees fit for you.

You realise that the mind cannot mess around with your self-image because every moment of your life you are moving, anchored in recognition of your *mool* – the destination of our journey in human form to achieve a blissful state (*anand*) and be in harmony with all creation. And this is the essence of *simran*, the unbroken connection with the light or *mool* within.

Simran begins as practising, practising and practising acts (*ghuns*) of compassion and love (*sewa*). The next step is to use the Guru's teachings (*gian*) to skip over sharp stones (suffering) and blunt stones (happiness) on your journey. Use these different stones (experiences) to build a staircase to reconnect with your *mool*.

Accept every experience you have with thanks and grace, and see them as opportunities provided to learn and propel yourself forward to your *mool* (*Jo Vartaie Sai Jugath Nanak Woe Kahaai Jeewan Mukath*). Such is the state of the *gurmukh* – always balanced, neither overly jumping with joy nor wallowing in sadness (*sehaj*). This is how you sing Guru Ji's praises. How you anchor in *anand*.

One of the highest qualities is to be grateful. When we meditate on being grateful, we have to not only extend it to the good but be grateful for the downs as well. I know this sounds hard or impossible, but this state is known as *chardikalah*, always seeing the good – either in intention or impact. Guru Gobind Singh best illustrated this when he was told that all his sons had been martyred, and the Singh who told him broke down in tears. The Guru replied, "Do not weep; I have thousands of children" – in reference to you and me. The devotee has to become like the infinite himself, and this is expressed in a *shabad* in the Guru Granth Sahib:

> *Hari harijan dou ek hain. Bib vichar kichh nahi. Jal te upaj tarang jio. Jal hi bikahi samai.* ("God and the servant of God are alike; there is no difference between the two. As the wave emerges from water and again merges into it, so does the soul merge in Union with God.")

This is *anand* – when you recognise your own *mool* as the infinite.

Chapter 6

Shine and Live as the Spirit

Jaisaa Saevai Thaiso Hoe. Nar Nihakaeval Nirabho Naao.

"You are moulded in the form of what you adore (Guru). He, makes you pure and fearless". *(SGGS)*

We live near Heathrow airport and the M4 and other main roads, and need to get the windows of our house cleaned every couple of months. You won't believe the black muck that comes off planes, cars and other vehicles. It lands on everything in the vicinity. You do not notice it until you run your hand along your car or any other surface. I can only guess what it does to your lungs.

Our regular cleaner retired earlier this year. He was an elderly Irish man who loved his coffee, chocolate biscuits and chatting. The thing I remember him most for is that he always recalled where he had left off our last conversation and picked it up from the same point. It is an amazing gift to have. He recommended we use the services of another gentleman for window-cleaning.

We have new cleaners now, a couple of young Bulgarians who initially struggled with their English but now, months later, have become quite fluent. They love their coffee, chocolate biscuits and chats, too. You get to know them quite well over time. We got talking about what I was doing recently, and I mentioned writing this book and what it was about. One of them said, "You must read books by Dan Millman". I had never heard of him but, after a quick search on Google, found out more about him.

Millman is an author of a series of books, including *The Way of the Peaceful Warrior*, which was made into a film starring one of my favourite actors, Nick Nolte. I didn't buy the book but did the next best thing – I watched Millman's video on YouTube. At the end of the presentation, he says something that really hit home:

> Now breathe and relax. Life comes to us in waves of change. We cannot predict or control those waves. But we can be better surfers. Practise and learn to be better surfers to manage the waves of change now and in each moment. Then the quality of the moment becomes the quality of our lives.

Thank you, my Bulgarian friends – *sangat* speaking and guiding me again.

Dan has captured and expressed the way I live my life now. If one is to succeed in anything, the success must come gently, with a great deal of effort but with no stress or obsession. To surf successfully, you have to understand the water and let go of the fear; you need to invest in a good surfboard and learn to surf – it is all about balance. You have to learn to trust yourself and to let go. Now you can have fun.

Death and the realisation of its inevitability have become my constant companions and advisors. I know I am never alone. All that touches me in every moment of my life has meaning. When the English poet William Blake (1757–1827) said, "Eternity is in love with the productions of time", perhaps he meant that we are never alone. I have become more "aware" of my inner self and my surroundings. I experience the connections effortlessly. I am not at the mercy of mood swings. There is a quietness in the mind and a strength in my shoulders to carry forth any challenge that life has in store for me. As Saint Augustine, whose writings influenced Western Christianity and philosophy, said, "Lord, I pray not for a lighter load but stronger shoulders".

Reading *The Journey to Ixtalan* recently, I came across something that I wholeheartedly relate to. Don Juan says:

> Death is our eternal companion – it is to the left at an arm's length. Death gives little warning; it comes with a chill. It is always watching you until it taps your shoulder. How can we feel so self-important when we know that death is stalking

us? The thing to do when you feel impatient is to turn to the left and ask death for advice. All acts of pettiness drop when you catch a glimpse of it or if you feel your companion is there, watching you. Death is the only best advisor we have. Whenever you feel that everything is going wrong and that you are about to be annihilated, turn to your death and ask if that you are wrong. Death is the hunter, always to the left, drop the petty thoughts, as if death would never touch them. Move around without attaching any intellectual meaning to anything. Feel the presence of death around you.

How profound are these words? Can we really waste our breath and time on things that don't matter, that don't contribute to our well-being? Can we really afford to live in the past, plan for the future at the expense of missing the richness and the opportunities of this moment? Don Juan makes this interesting observation:

For me the world is weird because it is stupendous, awesome, mysterious, unfathomable; my interest has been to convince you that you must assume responsibility, for being here in this marvellous world, in this marvellous desert, in this marvellous time. I want to convince you that you must learn to make every act count, since you are going to be here for a very short while, in fact too short for witnessing all the marvels of it.

Sadly, often when we speak of death, the usual reaction is one of fear. I prefer not to think of death as the end from which there is no coming back, but as a friend, a guide who gently reminds me of what is really important in every action taken and every thought had and given attention. It provides me with an anchor, keeping me grounded in the moment and allowing me to gently rock and marinate in the present moment, stopping me from drifting to the future or slipping away to the past.

Jean Paul Sartre, a French philosopher, and other key figures in the philosophy of existentialism and phenomenology describe fear as "the other is hell". It describes your experience of how often you want to escape from the "other", as if it is the source of all your troubles. Fear always involves the other; if somebody can take something away from you, this destroys your security. It includes death and illness; both are the other. Osho, an Indian mystic and philosopher also known as Rajneesh, in his translation of the Sikh scripture, the *Japji Sahib*, explains how the Sikh Gurus show the way of escaping the fear of death. "The only way is to seek the ONE, then no other remains. Then all fear fades away. There is no death, there is no illness; there are no inconveniences, because there is no other."

I had been given a new chance to experience life. I certainly did not want to go back to what I had been doing before the heart attack. I had to find something that would feed my soul as well as my body, in that order. As I struggled with this dilemma, I came across the following passage by Osho:

> Each person comes into this world with a specific destiny; he
> has something to fulfil, some message has to be delivered,
> some work has to be completed. You are not here accidentally;
> you are here meaningfully. There is a purpose behind you.
> The whole intends to do something through you.

But how do you find the right path that is meant for you? I tried writing a list of what I would enjoy doing. I spoke to family and friends. The list quickly filled up with grand schemes to change the world. Deep down, I was still seeking recognition through the kind of work I would do. This went on for months and I started to lose focus. My frustration was visible for everyone to see.

At the time, my daughter, then only 14 and an ardent student of karate, showed me *A Book of Five Rings: The Classic Guide to Strategy* by Miyomoto Musashi. I did not pay much attention to it at first. However, a few weeks later, out of sheer boredom, I picked it up and flipped through it. One passage in particular caught my attention:

> Even if you strive diligently on your chosen path day after day,
> if your heart is not in accord with it, then even if you think you
> are on a good path, from the point of view of the straight and
> true, this is not a genuine path. If you do not pursue a genuine

path to its consummation, then a little bit of crookedness in
the mind will later turn into a major warp. Reflect on this.

This added a bit of direction and focus to my quest, but I still had
to discover my path, my destiny. I realised that I had always been a
creature of habit and routine. I had somehow to stop these habits
and disrupt my routines. Easier said than done. Everything we do
is a routine, and this has become the source of our worry. Our life
is lived as a pattern. You get up at the same time, go about your
personal hygiene in the same order, eat meals at set times, and so
on. Try eating your breakfast half an hour later, and notice how you
keep on checking your watch or "likes" on Facebook for something
you posted. You get irritated and stressed. You live a life of moods.

Even as I did *sewa* and *simran*, I noticed patterns and habits
developing – for example, meditating at the same time in the same
position and the same chair, and looking at the watch to see if the
"allotted" time of one hour for the practice was over. Even when I
went to the temple to do *sewa*, it had to be at the same time and
the same *sewa*. It was as if taking ownership of the routine was
important rather than the act itself. We train ourselves to work with
external signals, triggered by habits and fulfilled by carrying out
the associated patterns. We become predictable. And that stops us
living a life of spontaneity and serendipity. And that is how we come
to the end of our lives – chasing our own tail and never catching it.
Habits are difficult to change. Here are a few words of wisdom on
the subject.

> "Habit is habit and not to be flung out of the window by any
> man, but coaxed downstairs a step at a time." Mark Twain,
> *Pudd'nhead Wilson*

> "Nothing is stronger than habit." Ovid (43 BC–17 AD), *Ars
> Amatoria*

> "The chains of habit are too weak to be felt until they are too
> strong to be broken." Samuel Johnson (1709–84)

> "How use doth breed a habit in a man!" William Shakespeare
> (1564–1616), *The Two Gentlemen of Verona, Act 5, Scene 4.*

Don Juan provides very good advice to Carlos Castaneda as he teaches him to be a hunter in *The Journey to Ixtalan*. He advises:

> A good hunter knows the routines of its prey. That is what makes you a good hunter. To be a hunter is not just to trap game, he is not a good hunter because he knows the patterns of his prey, but ... because he has no routines. This is his advantage. He is not at all like the animals he is after, with routines and predictable quirks. He is free, fluid and unpredictable.

As Don Juan teaches Castaneda how to hunt, he provides a valuable insight into how to be free and fluid. He says:

> In order to be a hunter you need to disrupt the routines of your life. Don't be like your prey – easy to predict. All of us behave like the prey we are after – that makes us a prey for something. The hunter should stop being a prey himself. Deer are difficult to catch because they have no routines. He [the deer] is aware of the routines and behaviours of ordinary hunters. A hunter will never walk into a forest without first considering his points of protection.

As I slowly learnt to be more attentive, an awareness of being aware developed. Deliberately, I began to break my routines. It was not easy; even the simplest actions you do all day are out of habit. I began with very simple things. Putting on the left sock before the right, untucking my shirt, sitting on a different chair, eating when hungry and not according to the clock. It sounds silly but, slowly but surely, I began to become spontaneous. There was no schedule to meet, no pattern to follow, and old habits just faded away.

This was liberating and it felt as if a big weight had been lifted off my shoulders. It felt right. I didn't have to be somewhere, be busy doing something, be going somewhere. It was liberating. A space was created within me that filled with appreciation and love for myself and the people and world around me. I realised that to know myself I did not need attention, just a sense of being aware.

As already mentioned, we have thoughts at the rate of one every 1.9

seconds. That is how busy we are in the head. These thoughts are mostly about the past and the future. But the past is gone and the future is still to come. You have no control over either – not that you have control over thoughts about now.

The egoistic mind is always seeking, striving and struggling and is driven by thought (which happens in time and space) that is influenced by knowledge of the past, the present, and the effects of perceptions of the future on the present. Thought that says "me", the egoistic mind, must control what is happening now and analyse, suppress or fulfil it (Jiddu Krishnamurti).

In short, thought that is time and space bound acts on incomplete information driven by the "me" of the egoistic mind. In the words of the eternal Sikh Guru (SGGS), mankind is sleeping and dreaming, and caught in an illusion (the illusion of the self caused by thoughts of the "me") and needs to "wake up".

The mind has to be stilled in order to create a space within each of us that creates awareness rather than more thoughts. Guru Nanak, the first Sikh Guru, points out that being in solitude is not stillness as your thoughts are always with you. There is a stillness created by thought which says "I must be still, I must be quiet, I mustn't hear," but is still based on noise. The Sikh strives for inward stillness while being in the human body, which is time and space bound; a stillness not dependent on anything. The absolute silence of the mind can see that which is eternal, timeless and nameless. This is meditation. (Jiddu Krishnamurti).

You must also learn how to stop your internal dialogue at will. As I changed my habits and patterns of going about my daily life, it became clear that there was an internal conversation (no, I am not mad, although others may disagree) going on inside me. It is as if one is talking to oneself. You have to stop and let this sink in, and you will realise that it is happening within you, too. I agree with Don Juan when he says that the internal dialogue is what grounds us. The world is such and such or so and so only because we talk to ourselves about it being such and such or so and so.

He further points out that, whenever the internal dialogue stops, the world collapses and extraordinary facets of ourselves surface, as though they had been kept heavily guarded by our words. You are like you are because you tell yourself you are that way. You are too heavy and self-important. Let go!

I had used the tools of *sangat*, *sewa* and *simran* to let go. These practical steps began to help me slowly drop my self-importance and strip me of years of conditioning that had provided me with a false identity. I stopped feeling righteous, conceited and wise. I felt ashamed of the way I had previously led my life. Not self-pity, but real shame about the falsity of how I had lived. I finally took responsibility for all my actions and decisions in the past. It wasn't somebody else's fault. I had arrived at this point in life because of my own actions and decisions.

Believe me when I say that, when this realisation sinks in, forgiveness follows. And then the heart fills with love and every decision and action you take from that point forward is soaked in love.

Consider the following maxims:

> "The glory of Christianity is to conquer by forgiveness." William Blake

> "Since love grows within you, so beauty grows. For love is the beauty of the soul." St Augustine

> "If a thing loves, it is infinite." William Blake

> "O Holy Spirit, descend plentifully into my heart. Enlighten the dark corners of this neglected dwelling and scatter there Thy cheerful beams." St Augustine

> "And we are put on this earth a little space that we might learn to bear the beams of love." William Blake, *The Little Black Boy*.

> "What does love look like? It has the hands to help others. It has the feet to hasten to the poor and needy. It has eyes to see misery and want. It has the ears to hear the sighs and sorrows of men. That is what love looks like." St Augustine

But I had to nurture faith first. The French writer Romain Rolland (1866–1944) wrote that "faith does not mean a blind acceptance; it has degenerated among downtrodden races, but rather a living and seeing institution". Faith becomes unshakeable when we have actually tried and tested the spiritual teachings. Then it becomes unshakeable and stays with us every moment of our lives. And this requires patience and perseverance. It takes time to understand.

Although I have a long way to go and have drawn inspiration and guidance from many who have followed the path, I believe that, with time as His grace fills the emptying vessel, my journey will become easier. As I walk on this path, I take comfort from the following *shabad*.

> *Charan saran guru ek painda jae chal. Satguru kot painda aagay hoi layt hai.* ("If you walk one step towards God, God advances hundreds of steps to welcome you.")

I can only conclude that there is no other purpose in life than to go on a journey of discovery that takes you to the recognition of the all-powerful pure, infinite spirit which each and every one of us is, but hidden under layers of conditioning. You have to peel these layers away and get to the core.

> *Moolu chhodi laage doojai bhaaee.* ("Abandoning the *mool*, you become attached to the love of duality.") (*SGGS*)

You can have an ambition about being the best doctor, engineer or artist in the world, and you may even convince yourself that you were born with a talent to do just that. Yes, you will be happy and content for a while, but my experience has shown that these are all short-lived and that you unwittingly keep on adding more and more weight on your shoulders until you become overwhelmed.

Don't get me wrong. We should have ambition and do exciting things – after all, you are the Creator himself – but let this ambition be guided and nurtured by your spirit and not your imagined identity.

> *Mool n boojhai aapanaa vasatu rahee ghar baari.* ("One who does not understand the *mool*, his real wealth remains undiscovered within his heart.") (*SGGS*)

When you do, you will not only prosper but also have a life of permanent contentment, what the Sikh Gurus call *sahaj*.

> *Moolu pashhaanani tin nij ghari vaasaa sahaje hee sukh hoee.*
> ([Those who] understand their own *mool* dwell within the home of their inner being [*nij ghar*] in peace and sahaj.")
> (*SGGS*)

Sahaj is when you go about doing whatever you do in your natural state, whatever the outcome, without expectation or demand, safe in the knowledge that everything that happens will be what is best for you.

Spontaneity and serendipity replace habits and patterns in your life. In this state, your life happens to you, you don't make it happen.

> *Oupadesu sunahu tum gursikhahu sachaa ihai suaaou:* ("O Gur-Sikhs! Listen to the teachings. This alone is the true purpose of life.") (*SGGS*)

We suffer because of spiritual ignorance. Guru Ji's message is simple: get rid of your spiritual ignorance and realise that you are the *mool*, the spirit – completely detached from your body and thoughts.

Karma and *samsara* are an integral part the Guru Ji's teachings. *Karma* simply means that every action has a consequence ("As someone sows, so he reaps" – *Bhai Gurdaas Vaaran*, p. 1). *Samsara* is the cycle of reincarnation ("Those who come, must go in the end; they come and go, regretting and repenting." *SGGS*). From every experience of suffering there is a lesson to learn. Suffering provides learning for spiritual growth.

We are infinite souls who have taken on a temporary form for a limited time. Next time you feel you are suffering, think about Guru Arjan Dev Ji (the first Sikh martyr, 1563–1606) sitting on a hot plate with burning sand being poured on him, singing "Your actions seem so sweet to me. Nanak begs for the treasure of the Naam, the Name of the Lord" (*SGGS*). That should provide some perspective.

Chapter 7

The Sikhs and their Gurus – The saint-soldier

Kar Kar Vaekhai Keethaa Aapanaa Karanee Kaar Karaaeidhaa

("Having created the gifts of existence and creation we are nurtured and guided to flourish.") (*SGGS*)

The Sikhs believe in one immortal being who is the Creator of the universe and resides within each and every aspect of His creation. God is omnipotent and omniscient.

The SGGS contains the *shabads* (the Guru's wisdom) that guide the Sikh practitioner to the timeless (Waheguru, God, Akaal.). The SGGS was first compiled by the Fifth Sikh Guru, Arjan Dev, in 1604 and finalised by Guru Gobind Singh in 1705. Besides the *shabads* of the various Sikh Gurus, it also includes *shabads* from various Hindu (of various castes) and Muslim saints. The message that is reiterated in the SGGS is that "awakening" – the realisation of God – does not depend on caste or on performing prescribed rituals or being an ascetic. Rather, it depends on meditating upon the *naam* (the virtues of the Creator reflected in the various names assigned to Him – Waheguru, Ram, Allah etc.), in the midst of life's responsibilities and turning from the body-mind (ego), towards the recognition of one's true identity – the creator himself. These virtues, amongst many others, include the practice of compassion, dharma, contentment, forgiveness, patience, fearlessness, humility and unconditional love. When one has the same virtues as the creator, then there is no separation between the Sikh and his Guru. They become One (EK).

Eleanor Nesbitt, the author of "*Sikhism: A Very Short Introduction*", 2005, provides a chronological comparison between the lifetimes of the Sikh Gurus (1469 to 1708) and the reign of the Mogul emperors from Babur, who ruled India from 1526, to Aurangzeb, who died in 1707. The actions of these rulers directly affected the Sikh Gurus.

The word "Sikh" implies a seeker of new knowledge (a learner, a disciple of the Guru), who is on a journey of the mind to discover the timeless. In other words, it is a journey that takes the Sikh from the *sargun* (the body mind) to pure consciousness *(nirgun)* and beyond that, to the pure timeless form *(Akal Purakh)*. More popular language descriptions refer to the same path of discovery as the movement from the body-mind towards awareness and finally to the witness of it all. This journey can only be completed with the grace of the Guru (SGGS), who guides the follower to move from darkness to light (*gu* = darkness; *ru* = light). This grace is referred to as *gurprasad*.

The follower who listens to and follows the teachings of the Guru is referred to as a *Gurmukh* (a person who is facing the Guru), and a person who does not follow these teachings is referred as *manmukh* (one who follows his own mindset). These terms apply only to individuals of the Sikh faith and are in no way applicable to followers of others. The Sikh Gurus were very vocal about the freedom of all religions to practise their faith as directed by their own Gurus.

The ten Sikh Gurus, who lived over a period of 239 years, and now embodied in the SGGS, systematically guide disciples, through the implementation of a number of tools, to the discovery of their true nature. These have been presented in the previous chapters as *sangat, sewa, ardhas, jap and simran*.

Very briefly, the first Guru, Nanak Dev ji, spread the True Word of God and made four long journeys over a period of 35 years, walking over 30,000 miles with his companions Bala and Mardana. He travelled in all four directions and visited the religious centres of Hindus, Muslims, Buddhists, Jains, Sufis, Yogis and Siddhas. He carried on open discourse with followers of these religions in order to spread his message of universal love and brotherhood, highlighting the futility of rituals, ascetic lives and caste systems in realising the creator (the *Akal Purakh*).

The second Guru, Angad Dev ji, introduced *Gurmukhi,* literally meaning "from the mouth of the Guru", as a written and spoken language rather than using the Hindu scripts such as Sanskrit, which was restricted for use by the priestly Hindu class. The Gurus did not believe in this elitism.

The third Guru, Amar Das Dev ji, promoted the equal rights of women and started the common kitchen, where everybody had to sit together for *lungar* (free food) regardless of caste or creed, thus dismantling the shackles of the prevalent practices of the caste system.

Ram Das ji, the fourth Guru, established the now Golden Temple, with four doors each facing towards a compass point to depict the freedom of all faiths, castes and communities to enter the temple and practise *dharam*. The temple also served as a centre for teaching Sikh values and participative community building. This was also the first step towards building strong institutional structures.

The fifth Guru, Arjan Dev ji, compiled the first copy of the SGGS, incorporating the teachings of all the previous Gurus and like-minded Hindu and Muslim saints. He was martyred by the then Mogul emperor, Jahangir, because people were becoming persuaded by Guru Arjan's teachings.

The sixth Guru, Hargobind Sahib ji, introduced the concept of *miri* (temporal power) and *piri* (spiritual authority), with the concept of *piri* always commanding the *miri*.

Siri Har Rai ji was the seventh Guru, and emphasised the importance of recognising and portraying one's true self and looking after the environment, while the eighth and youngest Guru, Har Krishan, showed through his work and wisdom that the attainment of full consciousness was not age-related and that enlightenment could be achieved by anyone, young or old.

The ninth Guru, Tegh Bahadar ji, was martyred by the Mogul emperor, Aurangzeb, to stop the persecution of other faiths, while the tenth Guru, Gobind Singh ji, formalised the Sikhs into the *Khalsa* (the pure) through an initiation ceremony that built the character of the Sikh to stand up to oppression with courage and determination, and to live in freedom and dignity without fear of persecution. Once the *Khalsa* army was ready, the tenth Guru passed the Guruship to the SGGS after adding compilations of the teachings of the ninth Guru.

The Sikhs had learnt in the religion's infancy that human freedom needed to be jealously guarded. History has recorded many Sikhs who laid down their lives willingly for the principles and beliefs that they held dear and those dictated by their living Guru, SGGS.

The purpose of the human race is to achieve a blissful state and to be in harmony with the earth and all creation. For spiritual beings, all that exists is sacred.

This year, 2017, Sikhs around the world celebrate 350 years of the *parkash* of Guru Gobind Singh, and find inspiration and guidance for living from the following two *shabads* penned by him. They signify the search for justice, equality and equity from a position of unconditional love by becoming the *santh-shipahi* – the saint-soldier or warrior-saint. Each exists because of the other. Neither can exist without the other.

The first shabad is *"Sach kahon sun leho sabai jin prem kio tin hee prabh paio"*. It's about loving the spirit; the Creator; our spirit; all creation. But how do we recognise and fall in love with God? The Guru, our *mool*, the place of love, guides us to find answers to our questions. Through the practice of *jap*, *simran*, *sewa*, the company of the *sadh sangat* and *ardhas*. These natural disciplines lead to recognition of the spirit within and its oneness with creation. You realise that the spirit within, the *mool* and all that is outside, are one. There is no separation of "me" and "other," and therefore no place for doubt, fear or hatred. This path of discipline, compassion, service, *sangat* and prayer develops the qualities of a saint. Only unconditional love remains.

The second shabad is *"Sawa lakh se ek ladaun, tabe Gobind Singh Naam kahaun"*. This is about having the strength and courage to fight the many challenges and battles of life. Moment by moment. Day by day. Plagued by thoughts every few seconds. Thinking about the past, the present, the future. The mind wants to control. Society wants to control. People in authority want to control. People you love want to control. Through faith and devotion, the Guru builds our character to face all these challenges and to keep us steadfast on our journey of discovery. A character of fearlessness, forgiveness, resolve, determination, integrity. The character of the warrior.

The *santh-shipahi*, the saint-soldier, has the love and character of the Guru. The soldier lives for *sarbat da bhala* by defending justice, freedom and equality for all. This is leadership through service, by speaking truth to power and through deeds as well as words. Honour Guru Gobind Singh Ji. You have his example. Aspire and reach to embody the *sant-shipahi*. Be complete; this is how you were born.

Remember all the battles you have already won and the fears you have overcome. However small, take the next step. You know where you are now. Get closer to where you want to be.

The journey begins with the limitless universe we experience and ends with the One we realise we are. *Naam, shabad, bani, hukam, maya, on-kar, mool, jyot, Guru,* you,me, are all, but *Ek* (One). Celebrate that. Be that. Now. In this moment. Be the *Aad Sach Jugaad Sach Haibhi Sach Nanak Hosi Bhi Sach.* We have always been that. Limitless, timeless. Pure love and pure intelligence.

Chapter 8

Learning that comes from the practice of acquired knowledge

Kabeer Saachaa Sathigur Kiaa Karai Jo Sikhaa Mehi Chook.

("Kabir, what can the True Guru do, when his disciples are at fault and do not practice the teachings"). (SGGS)

I have recently experienced some discomfort in my jaws upon exertion. Suspecting angina, I have undergone tests to establish the condition of my heart. These began with an angiogram, an echocardiogram next and, finally, an MRI. As a precaution, in the meantime I was put on a wonderful drug to improve the blood flow to the heart.

It's 7 February 2017, and my wife and I are sitting in the cardiologist's office discussing the final results of my tests. As we wait for the specialist in the Rapid Response Heart Unit of the Cardiology department, an angel in the disguise of a specialist nurse, Agnes, shares a beautiful experience with us. The previous night, at her house, an orchid had blossomed after a long time with a delicate purple flower. But it was on a branch that was slanted. She and her husband decided to tie the branch to a supporting stick. That was fine, but when she tried to straighten the branch, the flower just fell off.

Be patient – this has a bearing on my results. I like creating suspense; I'm told it's important to hold the reader's attention.

As the nurse finishes relating her experience, she picks up my test results and explains that there is significant damage to the area where the heart attack occurred. The damaged artery is heavily calcified.

The artery could be cleared and a stent inserted to improve the blood flow to the area. But there are obvious risks. And the doctors are not sure it would improve my symptoms related to angina. I am asked if I still have pain in the jaw since I have been on new medication. No, I reply emphatically, there is no pain upon exercising.

The cardiologist walks in and asks, "What do you want to do? Do you want to go ahead with the procedure or just manage the condition with medication?" I think about the delicate purple flower in full bloom, falling lifeless when forced out of its natural rhythm. I do not hesitate; the answer had already been provided. I just had to listen and learn.

"No procedure for me, sir", I reply. "The medication works well."

"Wise choice," replies the doctor. "I would have done the same in your shoes."

Nature, the Creator, *sangat* has spoken to me through the orchid, through the nurse, through the cardiologist.

How and what we learn is important. But more important than the gathering of knowledge is what we do with it. Our practice of it. The learning that comes from practice must help one take further steps towards discovering one's *mool*. It is not how much you know, but what you do with it that is important. Practice, practice is the message; don't just be a hunter-gatherer. We have limited time. You can be called back by your maker without a moment's notice. Change, and enlightenment comes slowly. Idries Shah, an author and teacher in the Sufi tradition known by the pen name Arkon Daraul, said "enlightenment must come little by little, otherwise it would overwhelm the seeker".

The "learning by doing" (*sewa, simran, jap*) takes us gently towards experiencing the eternal light (*mool*) within us and in all that exists. Don't just read and be critical of religious teachings. Stop the practice of rituals as they become the focus of your prayer and attention. Seek beyond, with the "spectacles" of Guru Ji's teachings, and the practice of them. Practice and change, be steadfast, do not waver (*Sawa Lakh sa Ek Ladaun*), and Guru Ji does the rest. From this blessing, the mind (*maan*) has total freedom to react spontaneously as opposed to being "boxed" (in rituals). One adapts to what the situation calls for, not believing in a system or a method (process) of doing things.

The SGGS always nudges us towards developing an experiential (through *sewa, sangat, simran*) understanding of the universe and all that exists within it (all is the light, the *jyot*). Having this understanding is freedom, which is but an expression of endless love. Guru Ji provides this understanding (the *gian*) but you must have an earnestness, a hunger within you for this freedom. You just need to say "Yes, I am ready to be guided from the innermost place, I surrender myself to the supreme authority" (*ardhas*).

We are intuitive beings but somehow, in our conditioning (attachment to shifting identities), we have been trained to rely on process thinking, trying to figure things out and treating life as if it is a strategy. Instead, be clear to your true nature and be that. In such a state, there is a space that is unchanging (*anand*). Acceptance of the "what is" in every moment (*Aad Sach Jugaad Sach Haibhi Sach Nanak Hosi Bhi Sach*) means living without the sense of the need to control. No control means there is no conflict, as conflict is a result of thought that relies on personal agendas.

Have the right intentions to guide your actions and the right actions will deliver on your true intentions. We know we are at ease, happy and at our best when there is no pretending. Guru Ji says, "Why not surrender to this ... the real you ... your *mool*?" Surrender, so that you are open to possibilities, and open to being guided by what is meaningful – your true natural guidance. Have faith in the real you.

When intentions are different from actions, the mind gets busy inventing stories to avoid being caught out. This is very tiring, as continued effort is required to justify these actions. No matter how hard one tries, gradually the true intentions come to the surface. The result is misery.

When actions reflect your true intentions, you stand up tall, take responsibility and accept any outcome, happy in the knowledge that you did your best and that next time you will do even better. With such values, the mind becomes free to learn and keep trying.

Use the company of the *sangat* to remind you of this, and *simran* and *sewa* to practise these values. You do not need to try to get out of misery; you just have to surrender and remember that actions must come from true intentions. In this way, you open the gates of love. The Guru in you, and in all of us, begins to guide, protect and deliver. Then you enjoy "yourself".

Sangat ji, we make numerous choices and change paths so many times (constantly wanting more – *trishna*) that we get confused and lost. Make Guru Ji your constant guide (feel his constant presence – *baragi*) and live a life of peace and poise (be content with what you already have – *sehaj maath*).

We have become creatures of habit and live a life with specific patterns. There is a sequence to our day. Every minute is booked. We end the day by making another list. We have too many paths to tread (no focus - *doubda*), and each has to be walked or we think something may go wrong (we feel inadequate, incomplete, disappointed – *aasa narasha rahaa*).

Guru Ji teaches us to pause, take stock of our lives and decide for ourselves if our lives have meaning to them (stop and let go – *adol atmak vaasta*). Let Him be your guide to take you on a journey that takes you away from being a performer (living a life of concepts) towards a place deep within you where you find your *mool,* that is fearless, creativity itself, beyond knowledge, beyond judging, beyond physical death and pure intelligence. Blow away your ignorance and let go of all you have known. Success will follow without you losing yourself.

Sangat ji, our attention wanders all the time and we either miss, overlook or ignore the beauty of what we are experiencing in the moment. Guru Ji's message is always about living in constant awareness (alert and attentive – *ek kaagar chit*) and in a state of acceptance (the moment is as it is supposed to be – *sehaj vasta*).

We are intuitively curious and want to feel, grasp, explore and understand every experience we have. And that is wonderful, because we are a part of the universe created for the experience of all (Guru is the Creator, the creation and the experiencing of it all – *aap pravirath aap niravitathee aapae akath kathheejai).* To appreciate and to take care of. But somewhere in our lives, we began to feel separated from our source, the *mool*, and started following the mind (*maan*), which is never silent and always seeking attention, losing the beauty of the moment.

Instead of wasting time through discourse, talk, rituals and questioning (*kahia khathia na paiae*), become a *Gurmukh* through service to others (*sewa*), constant remembrance of the Guru within you (through acts of compassion, love, forgiveness – *simran*) and by quietening the mind through meditation (*jap*). Guru Ji says you are already that which you seek, the *mool* (it is already written – *antar pritam vasia dhur karam likhia kartar*).

"We are a feeling, an awareness encased here. We are luminous beings, and for a luminous being only personal power matters," explains Don Juan.

It is common knowledge that everything ages and changes. In the *shabad* which is recited when somebody dies, *alhaahanees*, Guru Ji explains that everything you see and do is temporary and fluid, and your experience of it has a time limit.

Your intentions and actions determine the quality of your limited stay in this world. We get so caught up in the roles we play that we start manipulating others to suit our desires. This only leads to temporary happiness until the next "fix". What you sow is what you reap. Give love and you get love back; be compassionate and feel it coming back; give hate and hate comes back.

So why not accept these rules and experience life by experiencing the Guru, your light, within you, and let His intentions (nurturing all with love) drive your actions (compassion, understanding, patience, empathy, forgiveness) to serve as He pleases. Place your faith in the hands of the Guru, accepting every experience as is, with grace and thanks.

Sangat ji, there is an unexplained mad rush to achieve goals and success, to get somewhere, to find love. Behind this rush is desperation. What if we don't make it? What if we do, but realise that it wasn't what we wanted? Do we, can we, start all over again?

How do I hold on to my achievements? In the end, we sell ourselves short and settle for much less than we are capable of.

We cling to life. The choices we make translate into habits and patterns. And anything that does not fit these feels unsafe, unsure. We have unwittingly constrained ourselves. We carry out a constant internal dialogue. It keeps us rational. So, we think. "I don't have a choice. I have responsibilities," we rationalise. "At least it pays the bills," we say.

There is another way to live is Guru Ji's message. By breaking these habits and patterns of thinking. To wake up to a greater reality. Full of inspiration. Free from self-made shackles. To lead a life of serendipity. Practise the Guru's teachings. Realise you are the spirit. Always compassionate, content, selfless, non-judgemental. Just love. Stop the internal dialogue. Don't cling to life. *Be* life, be the experience. No expectations. No pressure. You are the writer, director, actor and witness of your life.

"There is no reality except the one contained in us", explains Herman Hesse in *Steppenwolf*.

We are either being judged by others or, worse, ourselves. And it is constant. Never letting up. Measuring our worth against each judgement. Living in fear. Behaving and acting to please others. Or just to maintain the status quo. Whose life are you living? Whose judgement do you value the most, and why? Living becomes a task. A heavy, dragging force.

This is how we get caught in psychological traps of the mind. No matter the condition of your physical, mental or financial well-being, the Guru accepts you. Never holding a grudge, wiping your slate clean, lightening your load. Infusing you with the breath of life.

Infusing you with new vigour and freshness to lead a life without fear and full of love. To live a life of contentment while seeking your highest dreams and aspirations. But with a difference now. Not swimming against the current, but with the current of life. Experiencing joy in each moment. Accepting the outcome of each action with grace, knowing that your Guru is working on your behalf, ensuring an outcome that does not bring suffering. Not being judged.

Consider the following wise words.

> Ask of those who have attained God; all speak the same word. All the saints are of one mind; it is only those in the midst of the way who follow diverse paths. All the enlightened have left one message; it is only those in the midst of their journey who hold diverse opinions. (Dadu, 16th-century Indian saint)

And ...

> Is it not a fact that the three doctrines (of Taoism, Buddhism and Confucianism) may be three, but the Way is ultimately one? But that hasn't stopped the priesthood of later generations from sole devotion to their own sects and repudiation of others, causing the basic essentials of all three philosophies to be lost in false distinctions, so that they cannot be unified and end up at the same goal. (Chang Po-tuan, 11th-century Taoist master, *Introduction of Understanding Reality*)

There is only one truth – the Eternal Truth. We are the spirit. The Creator. To discover that is our purpose. In the book "I AM THAT" by Nisargatta Maharaj (author), translated by Maurice Frydman and edited by Sudhakar S. Dikshit, the following simple but powerful words provide insights, into who, we really are.

> That in whom reside all beings and who resides in all beings, who is the giver of grace to all, the Supreme Soul of the universe, the limitless being -- I am that. (Amritbindu Upanishad).

> That which permeates all, which nothing transcends and which, like the universal space around us, fills everything completely from within and without, that Supreme non-dual Brahman -- that thou art. (Sankaracharya)

> The seeker is he who is in search of himself. Give up all questions except one: 'Who am I?' After all, the only fact you are sure of is that you are. The 'I am' is certain. The 'I am this' is

not. Struggle to find out what you are in reality. To know what you are, you must first investigate and know what you are not. Discover all that you are not -- body, feelings thoughts, time, space, this or that -- nothing, concrete or abstract, which you perceive can be you. The very act of perceiving shows that you are not what you perceive. The clearer you understand on the level of mind you can be described in negative terms only, the quicker will you come to the end of your search and realise that you are the limitless being. (Sri Nisargadatta Maharaj)

Sangat ji, imagine always being joyous, content, without worry, light on our feet, respected and trusted by everyone we meet and touch. The SGGS says that is possible, because that is who we really are. That is the "truth".

Guru ji reminds us that we are the spirit in the body and not the other way around - a body with a spirit. Suffering happens because we associate everything we do with the mind and body. Life then becomes a race to get to some-"where", to become some– "one"

With the grace of Guru ji, be guided to live as the spirit, the mool. From this deep fountain of love and intelligence, we can use our body and mind to be dynamic and live in the experience of every moment and every breath. Fully aware, that all these experiences, are planned and executed by the Guru himself. This is *sahaj vaasta*. Letting go of the steering of life. We are already "here", we are already "one". We are life.

Sangat ji, how well do we really know ourselves? It is not uncommon to define ourselves by what we do, where we were born or how others perceive us. We feel more "ourselves" (secure), when we are in a particular place, situation or surrounded by those who are familiar. Even in spiritual matters, we have preferences - a particular gurdwara, a favourite ragi, giani etc.

In short, we are more comfortable with ourselves in situations, where have some sort of perceived control. The truth is that we don't have clarity all the time. There is a perceived separation between ourselves and that which is perceived as unfamiliar.

Bhagat Kabir, says that is not the case at all. Listen, understand and apply the wisdom of those who have discovered that all that exists, is One. There is no separation between us and others. No control is required. Ask Guru ji to give us humility. When we have humility, there is no need for more *gian* (divine knowledge). It come from within, where it has always been (*asi math deejay meray thakur, sada tudh dhiae*). Then we understand who we are. Always sure and never in doubt. "Be — don't try to become" advices Osho

I leave you with the following *shabad.*

ਇਉ ਕਹੈ ਨਾਨਕੁ ਮਨ ਤੂੰ ਜੋਤਿ ਸਰੂਪੁ ਹੈ ਅਪਣਾ ਮੂਲੁ ਪਛਾਣੁ ॥੫॥

("Thus says Nanak – O mind! Your *Saroopu* [nature, identity]
is *Joti* [Divine Light]. [O mind!] Recognise your *mool* [source,
jyot, origin ...] (*SGGS*)

What is stopping you from this realisation? Reflect on this. It is who you are. We all are. Have always been.